A Treasury of
Minnesota Tales

A Treasury of
Minnesota Tales

Webb Garrison

Rutledge Hill Press™
Nashville, Tennessee

A Division of Thomas Nelson, Inc.
www.ThomasNelson.com

Published by Rutledge Hill Press, a division of Thomas Nelson, Inc., P.O. Box 141000, Nashville, Tennessee 37214.

Typography by E. T. Lowe, Nashville, Tennessee

Library of Congress Cataloging-in-Publication Data

Garrison, Webb B.
 A treasury of Minnesota tales / Webb Garrison.
  p. cm.
 Includes bibliographical references and index.
 ISBN 1 -55853-663-9 (pbk.)
 1. Minnesota—Anecdotes. 2. Minnesota—Biography—Anecdotes.
 I. Title
 F606.6G37 1998
 977.6—dc21   98-49048
                      CIP

Printed in the United States of America.

02 03 04 05 06 — 6 5 4 3 2

Contents

Introduction
Young and Diverse

As a political unit between Canada and Mexico, Minnesota is an adolescent. Massachusetts, Pennsylvania, and even Georgia are old-timers by comparison. Yet among the fifty states, Minnesota is close to the top in diversity.

The Native Americans who flourished there long before the arrival of the French explorers and British fur traders welcomed as visitors many other tribesmen of diverse backgrounds who made pilgrimages to the red pipestone quarries. Ownership of the territory's land and water moved back and forth among European nations many times before the region became a part of the United States through the Louisiana Purchase. Its multicultural history is still obvious today in the state's population, which has been and remains as diverse in background as any in the nation.

Minnesotans have made the Land of Lakes notable for superlatives. Here is the foremost medical clinic of its sort in the world. Business and industrial enterprises that rank number one in their categories are flanked by the largest indoor shopping complex ever built.

Measured by some criteria, citizens of the state are the best read in the nation, some say because the long, cold winters give them many months in which to semihibernate with books and magazines and newspapers. (Thus this small volume should find a substantial audience!) It is in no sense comprehensive, as more than one hundred other subjects could have been treated. Many of them practically shouted, "Take me! Take me!"

Maybe because Minnesotans are so diverse, persons and events described in these pages range from the mythical, comical Paul Bunyan to a dead-serious president of the United

States, the Western world's most noted evangelist, and a Sioux leader whose reluctant leadership in war led to the biggest massacre of whites by Indians in U.S. history.

If you're a Minnesotan, whatever your geographical or ethnic or racial background may be, here's hoping you'll find new sources of pride in these chapters about your state and a few of its people.

Part 1
Mavericks, Strays, and Zealots

This photograph of a Northern Pacific express is labeled "Advance of Civilization."

1
Jim Root

A Railroad Record

Air pollution was not considered a problem in Minnesota in 1894; the ever-present smoke from "clearing fires" was simply a nuisance—or a sign of progress. Settlers and loggers pouring into the area's immense virgin forests kept the "clearing fires" going for days on end as they got rid of trees and brush for which they had no use. On many dry days, smoke could be seen and smelled almost anywhere in the state.

That's one reason citizens of the sawmill town of Hinckley paid little attention to the thick, blue haze they saw when they got up on the morning of September 1, 1894.

Promptly at seven o'clock the whistle of the big Brennan Lumber Company, the largest employer in Pine County, blew to announce that another day's work was starting. So much lumber went out that the remote town was linked with Saint Paul and Duluth by two competing railroads, the Eastern Minnesota, and the Saint Paul and Duluth Railroads.

At the Eastern Minnesota depot that morning a freight train that belonged to James J. Hill's Great Northern system stood ready to depart with its cargo of green lumber. Later in the day passenger trains would come both to this station and to that of the Saint Paul and Duluth Railroad. How important this transportation would soon become, no one dreamed during the midmorning hours.

Soon the blue-gray haze became so thick that payroll clerks at the sawmill had to light kerosene lamps. A sudden burst of wind-whipped flames from an old logging road sent sparks into the outskirts of the town. During the morning the volunteer fire department responded to half a dozen calls, each to a different site, but the firefighters had no difficulty bringing the blazes under control.

Shortly after 1:00 P.M., however, the situation took a dramatic turn. A telegraph message from the south reported that nearby Pokegama was "burning furiously and the town could not be saved." To a few observers, it seemed that the grayish clouds of smoke turned black in a matter of minutes.

Father Lawler, the only Catholic priest in the logging town, decided to take matters in his own hands. Waving his arms, he ran up and down the principal streets shouting in his deep, bass voice, "Forest fire! Run! Everybody run!"

Many struck out for the shallow Grindstone River at the edge of town. Others headed for a huge three-acre gravel pit that always held stagnant muddy water. At least seventy-five people hurried to the Eastern Minnesota Railroad station, where passenger train No. 4 was waiting along with freight train No. 23. With William Best at the throttle of engine No. 125 and fireman George Ford throwing coal into the boiler, the passenger train coupled with the freight, and refugees began crowding into the thirty empty boxcars ready to be rolled south behind the engine controlled by Best. No one knows how many Hinckley residents were aboard when the train pulled out, but the number may have exceeded six hundred.

As the last passengers crawled aboard, paint on both freight and passenger cars began to blister. Just as the now-lengthy train crossed the bridge over the Grindstone River, the structure's creosote-soaked timbers burst into flame. Best didn't dare stop, but he did slow down enough to enable some runners to jump aboard. Minutes later the hybrid train roared into Sandstone village, eight miles from Hinckley, with the boxcar refugees shouting out the news that "Pokegama has gone up in smoke, and Hinckley will be next."

Offered places on the already crowded train, the Sandstone residents and their families declined. They had lived through so many warnings of forest fires that they were in no mood to run. Not a man, woman, or child joined the refugees at Sandstone, so after a brief pause the motley train moved forward again. Twenty minutes later fire leveled every structure in Sandstone.

Meanwhile, back in Hinckley, those who had run to the Grindstone found that the river water was too shallow to give

In 1894, hundreds of thousands of acres were covered with virgin forests that included immense trees of several varieties. [WINSLOW HOMER, 1894]

protection except in occasional pools. At the gravel pit the situation was much worse, as the water covering its bottom was seldom more than four inches deep.

Singly and by families, residents who decided they couldn't survive if a real forest fire swept upon their places of refuge took to the railroad tracks. They walked or ran as long as their stamina permitted. If a place of safety could be found, it would have to be somewhere north of their town.

As the terrified Hinckley residents fled northward, Jim Root, at the throttle of passenger train No. 4 of the Saint Paul and Duluth Railroad, started his train southward at 1:50 P.M. Jerking its way out of the Duluth depot, engine No. 69—stoked by John McGowan—was making its scheduled run to Saint Paul. All four cars of the express train were unusually full, holding an estimated 150 passengers.

A long-time resident of Minnesota, Root was said to have been engineer of a hospital train that had transported hundreds of sick and wounded Union fighting men from the Andersonville prison at the end of the Civil War. During his twenty-three years as a Saint Paul and Duluth engineer, he had no blemishes on his record. Barely a quarter of an hour out of Duluth, the smoke was already so thick that he was forced to turn on the headlight of his locomotive and lean out of his cab to scan the track ahead. By the time the train was approaching Hinckley, Root admitted to his fireman that he doubted that they would be able to complete their run.

Two miles north of the station that was his next scheduled stop, Root saw a tousle-haired boy running barefoot toward the oncoming locomotive. A few yards behind the youngster, small groups of desperate men, women, and children were headed north as fast as they could go. Root ground his train to a halt and leaned forward to hear a stout woman cry, "Hinckley's burning! Half the town's dead!"

Originally known simply as Central Station because trains stopped there, Hinckley was a sparsely inhabited village until 1874 when entrepreneur Thomas Brennan established a sawmill there on the Grindstone River. Within a generation the mill employed more than three hundred men who thought nothing of cutting two hundred thousand feet of lumber during a single day.

Although sewers, electricity, and telephones had not yet come to the sawmill town, booming business at the Brennan Lumber Company persuaded investors to put fifty rooms into the Morrison Hotel when it was built there to accommodate drummers and lumber buyers. By 1890 Hinckley, the county seat of Pine County, had a population of more than six hundred, with twice that number of residents living outside its boundaries. Like Hinckley, the county's economy was rooted in lumber alone. Its 201 farms, scattered over many square miles and seldom larger than twenty acres in size, boasted just 200 horses, 300 mules, 400 hogs, 100 turkeys, and 57 ducks.

Like tens of thousands of other Minnesotans, many of those who lived in and around Hinckley had come from Scandinavia or had roots there, and their names reflected this: Annex Hedland, William Kpannenstiek, Gust Stenberg, Vilas Vick, Eric Scherstrom. The area's immense forests of firs, spruces, birches, and magnificent white pines served as magnets to draw newcomers to lumber camps. Any fellow willing to work could always find a job, but wages hovered below sixteen cents an hour.

Twenty years before Hinckley went up in flames, immense

quantities of lumber were coming from the region drained by the Saint Croix River and others like it. Villages whose names seldom appeared on maps used in the East were sources of badly needed lumber. Pine City, Hinckley, North Branch, and dozens of other communities figured only in invoices and correspondence about the ever-growing tide of lumber that flowed from their sawmills.

"Timber cruisers" who selected trees for cutting rarely marked a tree whose trunk was less than two feet in diameter. Smaller ones, often cut to get them out of the way, dropped to the floor of the forest and eventually began to rot. Huge quantities of brush accumulated wherever the axes of the woodmen were busy. This abundant source of fuel, coupled with windfalls, caused forest fires to become endemic and taken for granted.

Before the middle of the eighteenth century, a Catholic missionary had traveled from Grand Portage to the Lake of the Woods by canoe. His diary described smoke so dense that during the entire trip he did not get a single clear glimpse of the sun or the moon. More than a century later, Minnesota's first major *recorded* forest fire roared through Hinckley, burning at least sixty land sections and leaving an estimated 40,000 acres charred and blackened. Established in 1870, that record was shattered four years later when "the Hinckley fire" raced over an estimated 320,000 to 350,000 acres.

Neither Jim Root nor anyone else caught up in the inferno of September 1 had any idea of the size of the fire that threatened their lives. Before his train had fully halted that day in front of the escaping refugees from Hinckley, the railroad engineer shouted orders that enabled around one hundred of them to crowd aboard. Molly McNeil, age sixteen, was reputedly the last person to shove into the packed mass of humanity on the train.

"Can't make it to Hinckley," she is said to have panted to the brakeman. "The trestle over the Grindstone River is already on fire."

Word was relayed to Root, and the veteran railroader made a daring split-second decision. While a long whistle blast was still sounding, he threw engine No. 69 into reverse. Because he had been over the line scores of times, no one needed to tell him that there was no water closer than Skunk Lake—six miles

Although longer than his, this crack train is very similar to Root's. [BANK OF PORT JERVIS, NEW YORK, ENGRAVING.]

to the north. As his train shuddered backward, flames leaped through trees to the south at a speed estimated in excess of seventy-five miles an hour.

Such a burst was the result of heat buildup combined with a steady breeze from the south that blew at about twenty miles an hour. The flames seemed to leap and twirl and dart as though they were being directed by a frenzied demon. Root's engine had barely begun to gain a little speed before a blast of superheated air caught up with it.

When the flames caught up with the train, Root had turned sideways on his seat, an act that probably saved his life, for every pane of glass in his locomotive shattered simultaneously. Flying fragments cut into his neck, shoulders, and forehead. Many windows in the coaches were smashed at the same time. Cross ties blazed on both sides of the track, and the baggage car caught fire.

Wiping blood from his eyes, the engineer leaned far out of the window in a futile attempt to see which way the track led. As he peered to the rear of the train, the fire demon pounced on the unprotected cab with all of its fury. Root gasped and slumped over his hot throttle, unconscious. His shirt blazed, and the grimy side curtains of the locomotive vanished in a burst of flame.

McGowan, shielded from the worst of the blast, was not seriously injured. He grabbed a bucket and began dipping water from the tank of the locomotive to douse Root. As the engineer began to regain consciousness, he instinctively peered at the steam gauge. "God!" he moaned. "Just ninety-four pounds!"

Shifting the throttle to full open, he sent the train hurtling backward. It swayed and bucked but remained on the rails. Fire, meanwhile, seemed to be deliberately chasing the fleeing train. Flames scurried along the woodwork inside the cab and caused big blisters to pop up on painted surfaces. Soon even the coal in the tender was ablaze.

Root's hands swelled so much that the skin became tight and he could bend his fingers only with difficulty and agony. Several times new blasts from the pursuing inferno knocked him off his seat. He crawled back up to the controls so many times he lost count. Each time Root fell, McGowan threw water on him. Between forays into the front of the cab, the fireman retreated to his shelter and periodically emptied the bucket over his own head.

Accustomed to perils of what was then backwoods country, some people took the situation calmly. Passenger C. A. Vandever of Davenport, Iowa, tried to calm the conductor, who seemed crazed by the heat and danger. Dr. W. H. Crary of Saint Paul used his prescription pad to jot down notes—until the paper caught fire. But these men and others who showed no signs of fear were greatly outnumbered by riders who lost control of themselves. Molly McNeil saw one burly fellow give his wife a hasty kiss and then jump through a window. Two elderly Chinese, crouched near an open door, refused to move to a less-exposed spot; both burned to death where they knelt.

Half-sobbing, Root wiped his eyes again and again. He could see no more than four feet beyond the edge of the track, but what few landmarks he could see suggested that the train had reached Skunk Lake. When he began to brake, fires were blazing in every car. Frenzied passengers piled off before the train stopped and ran for the shallow water.

Those in the front of the frenzied crowd discovered that the lake was surrounded by a barbed-wire fence; men ripped the wire from the posts with their bare hands. Over two hundred people plunged into the slimy water that was less than eighteen inches deep.

Jim Root was too far gone to make it to Skunk Lake by him-

A cartoon of an imaginary interview between a railroad officer and a would-be brakeman. The officer tells him that at the present there is no vacancy, but by next week, death on the job will have created one. [HARPER'S WEEKLY, 1875]

self. McGowan and two other men pulled the engineer's hands from the throttle, gasping as they saw that the skin from his palms remained on the iron. Root's eyebrows were burned off, and most of his hair was gone. His face and the top of his head were covered with livid blisters.

There seemed little hope that he could live, but his fireman insisted on dragging him to the edge of the pond. Dawn found him unconscious but breathing. His massive engine was only twisted iron scattered along the track.

Root eventually recovered, so his name was not on the list of 418 casualties from Hinckley and half a dozen smaller villages. Many were buried in a mass grave, marked by a plaque that is dedicated to "The Pioneers of Civilization in the Forests of Minnesota."

Reacting to the Hinckley disaster, the state legislature enacted measures to "preserve the forests of this state and to prevent and suppress forest and prairie fires."

Despite praise showered upon him throughout the United States, Jim Root received no reward and lies in a grave marked by no bronze plaque. Yet the now-forgotten hero established a record that has yet to be matched.

Ignoring the long-standing code that a train should move backward only during switching, he had pushed his express No. 4 train northward at an estimated speed of eighteen miles an hour. By doing the unthinkable, Jim Root saved an estimated three hundred lives as he traveled in reverse to Skunk Lake. Now remembered chiefly by railroad buffs, his race against fiery death is without equal in the saga of the iron horse.

Today one of Hinckley's old railroad stations houses the Fire Museum that is the closest thing to a Root memorial. There the impact of a multimedia presentation, a mural, and photos is heightened by a display of partly melted household objects that were not completely destroyed on September 1, 1894.

Hinckley's Fire Museum at 106 Old Highway 61 is open daily from May 1 to mid-October. Telephone: 612-384-7338.

2

Lewis Cass

Treaty Maker

A big fellow of decidedly western appearance, with "the shoulders of an ox and the jowls of a bloodhound," Lewis Cass pushed into the offices of U.S. War Department. "Where do I find Calhoun?" he demanded of a clerk.

"Secretary of War Calhoun is in his office, sir, but his schedule is full for the day and he is occupied with official business. You may leave your name if you wish."

"If he wasn't occupied with official business, I would make a complaint," Cass snorted. "I haven't come all the way from Detroit to leave my name. Just march yourself to his office and tell him that Cass has arrived."

Five minutes later a subdued clerk signaled for the newcomer to follow him and said, "This way please, General Cass; Secretary Calhoun will see you at once."

South Carolina-born John C. Calhoun, destined to gain lasting fame as the framer of the nullification doctrine that led toward secession of the South in 1861, had a quick moment to review his correspondence with Cass before his visitor reached his office.

During 1819, Cass, the governor of the Michigan Territory, had repeatedly indicated that he'd soon come to the nation's capital "with a plan and an urgent request." Precisely what this plan and request might be, Calhoun had only a vague idea. In the light of the governor's background and experience, it was well within the range of possibilities that he might propose a punitive military expedition directed against the British in the region west of the Great Lakes.

A native of New Hampshire, Cass was known to have the

ear of Daniel Webster, who had been his schoolmate. After having migrated to Ohio, Cass entered politics, won a seat in the legislature at age twenty-four, and was outspokenly loyal to Thomas Jefferson.

Upon the outbreak of the War of 1812, the Buckeye-by-choice became colonel of the Third Regiment of Ohio Volunteers and fought under Gen. William Hull. Cass was on an expedition to the Raisin River when a courier brought news that Hull had surrendered his entire force at Detroit. Furious, the colonel announced that he would never surrender his sword to an Englishman or an Indian and promptly broke it, tossing the pieces to the ground.

Since the British had no way to transport all the men Hull had surrendered, Cass was given a parole and permitted to go to Washington. There his willingness to fight "anywhere at any time" brought him commissions as a brigadier general of volunteers and a colonel in the U.S. Army.

Upon expiration of his parole early in 1813, he joined William Henry Harrison to fight on the northwestern frontier. After having recaptured Detroit, jubilant Americans pushed British forces and their Indian allies into Canada. On October 5, 1813, Harrison and Cass routed their foes in the battle of the Thames River. When the dead were recovered from the field, one of them was the Shawnee leader Tecumseh.

That smashing victory in Canada had secured the Northwest Territory for the United States and propelled Harrison into national prominence that would eventually take him to the White House in 1841. Before the end of October 1813, Cass was rewarded by being made governor of the vast and largely unknown Michigan Territory, which was later expanded to include present-day Iowa, Minnesota, and portions of the Dakotas. Although the region included only a handful of Americans, it was the American center of the British-controlled lucrative fur trade.

When he came to Washington to see the secretary of war eight years later, Cass got down to business as soon as the two men had exchanged pleasantries. Emphasizing his arguments with forceful jabs of his big right fist, the governor proposed that an official expedition into the Northwest be mounted. He'd lead it personally, Cass promised. Queried concerning the object of such a trek, he leaned forward and responded,

His downturned mouth and sagging cheeks caused many people to compare Lewis Cass with a bloodhound.

"Though it is now a part of the United States, we know little about its geography north of the point where the Minnesota River flows into the Mississippi. The source of the Father of Waters lies somewhere in unexplored country, and I would very much like to be the man who discovers it, sir.

"There is a second consideration almost as important. We are in great need of treaties with the Indians of the Northwest, and my experience in such matters makes me uniquely qualified to lead the expedition that I have outlined."

Calhoun was familiar with the 1817 Treaty of Fort Meigs, whose terms demonstrated that Cass both yearned to "expand our national empire" and "knew how to deal with the red man." Cass had won the cession of their remaining Indian lands in Ohio and in parts of Michigan and Indiana.

Yet the secretary of war expressed surprise when his distinguished visitor informed him that an 1819 treaty signed at Saginaw was even more important than the earlier one. "The Chippewas with whom I parleyed at Saginaw eventually ceded immense tracts inside Michigan," he told Calhoun. "These lands have not been carefully surveyed as yet, but I am confident that they amount to some six million acres."

"Please accept my hearty congratulations," the secretary of war said. "There is a great deal of merit in your proposal, but you have not told me what you wish me to do to make it successful."

"Give me a few good men with scientific knowledge," Cass proposed. "I do not have the background and experience needed to make accurate geographical observations, and I know very little about such things as botany and geology. Surely there are such men at the War Department."

"Yes, but I cannot send them on detached service without the approval of President Monroe. Give me twenty-four hours to select suitable persons to become members of your expedition, then meet me at the White House late tomorrow afternoon."

Escorted through the Executive Mansion by Calhoun, Cass indulged in fantasy. *Someday,* he said to himself, *I may find myself sitting in Monroe's chair, waiting to receive important visitors . . .*

James Monroe listened as his secretary of war outlined the plan to learn more about the great Northwest and simultaneously to move the Indians out of it. "You are contemplating a very long journey," he commented to Cass. "How will you travel through the wilderness?"

"By canoe, Mr. President. An overland trip of this magnitude would not be possible; in much of the country I propose to survey, there are no trails." He hastily added his estimate that members of the expedition would travel five thousand or more miles during a journey that might last a full year. "Nothing is more important to the future than our firm acquisition of land," he urged.

Monroe nodded agreement; his absorbing interest in national expansion had helped him to become chief executive. Turning to Calhoun, he inquired if the War Department could furnish a few specialists to accompany Cass.

"If the governor of the Michigan Territory is willing to proceed with them, I can give him a pair of my best," Calhoun replied. "David B. Douglas has had extensive experience in making charts and is eager to go. And no man in the department knows more about mineralogy, botany, zoology, and such things than our Henry R. Schoolcraft, whose name is probably familiar to you, Mr. President."

Monroe nodded; during the four years he had occupied the White House, he had often heard Schoolcraft praised as a man of many talents. Extending his hand to Cass, he said that the

expedition would have his hearty blessing and full coopera-
tion. There was only one aspect of it that he wished to
emphasize.

"You have mentioned the making of treaties, and I am
delighted. The condition of the aborigines within our national
limits, and especially those who are within the limits of any of
the states, merits particular attention.

"Using force to remove these tribesmen from the territory on
which they now reside, even with a view to their own security
and happiness, would be revolting to humanity and utterly
unjustifiable. Between the limits of our present states and territories and the Rocky Mountains and Mexico there is a vast territory to which they might be invited with inducements that
might be successful."

Cass voiced support of the president's point of view, but he
said not a word about his personal conviction that "all Indians
must be sent somewhere far away—the sooner the better."
Without having met Douglas and Schoolcraft, he expressed satisfaction that they would accompany him.

"You will never regret your decision, Mr. President," he told
Monroe as they parted.

Much planning had been done earlier, but the organization of
the expedition took more time than Cass had expected. When
his little flotilla of canoes finally swung into Lake Superior on
the first leg of its long trek to what was then the Northwest, he
hoped that the journey would provide him with the finest hours
of his life. Although experienced outdoorsmen were in his company, it was the governor who every afternoon decided where
to make camp for the night. It took weeks to explore most of the
northern shore of Lake Superior, after which Douglas calculated
a course to take them almost due west.

Finally inside the region destined to become Minnesota, Cass
recorded his wonder at the majesty of Saint Anthony Falls in
what is now Minneapolis before turning his attention to details
of the portage around the falls. When they were a day's journey above the region that now constitutes the Twin Cities, he
pointed up the fast-dwindling Mississippi River and grunted,
"Push ahead, men, as fast as you can; we must not let winter
catch us here."

It took the expedition more than three weeks to reach a body
of water shown on no existing map, which the governor of

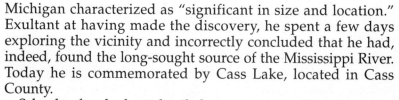

*While serving as U.S. secretary
of war, fiery John C. Calhoun
helped to sponsor the Cass
expedition into the Northwest.*

Michigan characterized as "significant in size and location."
Exultant at having made the discovery, he spent a few days
exploring the vicinity and incorrectly concluded that he had,
indeed, found the long-sought source of the Mississippi River.
Today he is commemorated by Cass Lake, located in Cass
County.

Schoolcraft, who kept detailed notes, was awed by the size of
the dense hardwood forests through which the party passed.
Once power was harnessed to sawmills, he expected fine oaks
and maples to float downriver in great numbers, he noted. But
since the expedition turned back toward the south and east upon
leaving Lake Cass, the scientist did not realize that they had
failed to reach "the Pineries," millions more acres covered with
the nation's finest white pines, firs, spruces, and Norway pines.

"Though numerous aboriginal tribes are represented in what
they call 'the land of sky-tinted water,'" he noted, "I believe the
Sioux are the most numerous and powerful."

After having examined numerous mineral outcroppings
with great care, the scientist recorded his conviction that the
region included high-grade iron ore in abundance. That obser-
vation proved to be correct, for more than two centuries later
Minnesota was known around the world as the source of at

A military victory propelled William Henry Harrison into the presidency and brought Lewis Cass the governorship of the Michigan Territory. [PARKER AND DITSON SONG SHEET]

least 60 percent of American iron ore. Schoolcraft was wrong, however, in believing copper to be nearly as abundant as iron. He also erred by a gross underestimate when he wrote, "For unknown reasons, the land seems to be dotted with lakes; there must be at least one thousand of them here."

Almost as interested in the region's flora and fauna as he was in its mineral resources, the War Department scientist recorded his wonder at the immense number of beaver, mink, elk, deer, moose, and black bears that he saw. Although raccoons, foxes, and bobcats were less numerous, they were still far more abundant than in "long-settled regions of the East," he observed. Schoolcraft also saw a great many pike and trout and lesser numbers of pickerel and perch in the streams and lakes. He carefully noted having seen "near two hundred different species of birds," and he speculated that fruits and berries to support bird populations "must undoubtedly come from extremely fertile land."

Cass and his followers seem to have spent a few days at the pipestone quarries that the Indians valued so highly. They then took a circuitous route to the south and west and after many weeks of hard travel reached a town with mud-filled streets that the residents called Chicago. An earlier traveler had characterized the place as "the desolation of dullness," but after having spent months in the region destined to become Minnesota, the governor of the Michigan Territory was enthralled by the fast-growing community.

He noted in his journal a conviction that Chicago would soon be a "large depot for inland commerce" as well as "a great thoroughfare for travelers."

Reporting to Washington at the end of his epochal journey, Cass said that he rejoiced at having found the source of the Mississippi River but was greatly disappointed at having concluded only two treaties during more than twelve months.

One of them, made near the falls on the Saint Marys River early in his voyage, required the Chippewas of the region to give up their ancestral lands. The second, framed at Chicago more than a year later, "brought to a satisfactory end the long process of extinguishing all Indian claims in Michigan south of Grand River." This time representatives of the Ottawas and Potawatamies as well as the Chippewas made their marks in obedience to gestures from the governor.

The explorer of Minnesota served as secretary of war from 1831 until 1837, during the administration of Andrew Jackson, and the "strange sense of foreboding" experienced in his visit to James Monroe took on new meaning when Democrats nominated him for the presidency in 1848. Later becoming James Buchanan's secretary of state in 1857, the governor-explorer took great pride in being hailed in Washington as "chief among treaty makers." His papers suggest that he framed at least twenty-two treaties gaining U.S. title to Indian lands, but critics assert that "he actually effected only nineteen treaties." Regardless of the actual count, few other military or political leaders laid the foundation for the removal of so many Indians to the West.

No one knows precisely how many millions of acres passed to the nation as a result of zealous treaty-maker Cass. One matter is beyond dispute, however. Pioneers who succeeded in making Minnesota a state in 1858 were grateful to the New Hampshire native and others like him. The official seal of the Gopher State includes a solitary warrior who rides westward toward the sunset. This figure is a symbolic reminder of the period in which "the land became truly American" as a result of forcibly expelling most native Americans from it.

His long and dangerous journey through Minnesota provided Cass with material to write several articles for the *North American Review* and for an 1823 volume called *History, Traditions and Languages of the Indians*. Few authors have had more pride in their work than the former governor of the Michigan Territory.

He was, however, deeply humiliated when geographers determined that the true source of the Minnesota-born Mississippi River lies about one hundred miles west of Lake Cass. Schoolcraft, who in 1821 had brought back a treasure trove of information about the Land of Lakes and its resources, returned to the region and in 1832 announced that the Father of Waters arises at Lake Itasca then flows through several glacial lakes before its confluence with the Minnesota River. Unlike sizable Lake Cass, these tiny lakes appear only upon highly detailed maps of large scale.

Although Cass was wrong in identifying Lake Cass as the source of the Mississippi, he was right in believing the Mississippi was an extremely important waterway. With its tributaries the Mississippi River system totals more than fifteen thousand miles in length and is by far the biggest in North America.

3

A Person Unknown

The Kensington Stone

8 Goths and 22 Norwegians on an exploration journey from Vinland far to the west. We camped by two rocky islands a one-day journey north of this stone. We were out fishing one day. When we came home we found 10 men red with blood and dead. AVM save from evil.

Using ancient phonetic symbols rather than the English shown here, someone chiseled that message into the face of a three-foot slab of graywacke stone (a fine-grained type of conglomerate) at an unknown time and place. Almost as though it were an afterthought, an additional sentence was chiseled into the edge of the six-inch-thick stone whose bottom surface shows markings that were cut into it by the movement of a glacier: "Have 10 men at the sea to look after our ships at a 14-day journey from this island. Year 1362."

Several stones bearing writings that seem to antedate the coming of Columbus have been found in North America. None of them, however, have achieved the fame of the slab found on a Kensington, Minnesota, farm. Except for the Rosetta Stone unearthed in Egypt by one of Napoleon's officers in 1799, the Kensington Stone is the most famous carved inscription to turn up in recent centuries.

Late in the fall of 1898, Olaf Ohman was eager to complete the clearing of a piece of ground so it could be planted the following spring. Aided by his young son and two or three hired hands, he used animals to pull one stump after another from the rocky ground. They ran into trouble, however, on the southern slope of a knoll that slanted toward the nearby farm

Only when viewed horizontally does the message carved into the side of the Kensington Stone become easily seen. [RUNESTONE MUSEUM]

of Nils Flaaten. The stump of a sturdy poplar of a variety that once abounded throughout vast tracts of Minnesota forests proved to be strangely stubborn.

Frustrated by the delay, Ohman brought all the animal power he had to the spot. When the roots finally gave way and the stump toppled onto its side, a member of the work party saw the source of their difficulty. The roots were firmly grasping a chunk of common graywacke. It is said that Ohman observed that the stone bearing chisel marks barely visible under the mud "might make a good doorstop."

Talk about the strange piece of rock that had turned up on the Ohman place reached the county seat in a matter of weeks. On January 1, 1899, Swedish-born J. P. Hedberg decided to try to find out what the odd symbols meant. Writing to editor Swan J. Turnblad of the Swedish-language *Svenska-Amerikanska Posten* newspaper in Minneapolis, Hedburg confided that something mighty queer had turned up in lake-dotted Douglas County.

Clearly interested, the newsman would have liked to see the stone for himself, but he didn't think it warranted a 250-mile round trip by horse and buggy. Instead he published the Hedburg letter, illustrated by the writer's rough sketch of the characters that had been found on the stone. Although the Kensington resident was not entirely accurate in depicting some of the characters, he correctly showed that 219 of them had been chiseled into Ohman's odd discovery.

After having published it, Turnblad turned Hedburg's pencil sketch over to Prof. O. J. Breda at the University of Minnesota. Having been born in Norway and having long been interested in ancient languages, Breda needed only one day to reach a conclusion. Most of the markings on the stone seemed to be very early *runes*, or alphabetic characters of ancient Germanic peoples.

On January 14, 1899, a translation of the stone's message— modestly characterized by Breda as "approximate"—was published in the university newspaper *Ariel*. A student editor appended to the story a conjecture that someday this piece of Minnesota graywacke might be displayed alongside the Rosetta Stone, which had provided scholars with the key to deciphering Egyptian hieroglyphics.

When the Breda translation was transmitted to readers of the *Svenska-Amerikanska Posten*, editors of several other Swedish-language newspapers picked it up. So did the prominent English-language *Chicago Tribune*.

An interested party whose name does not appear in newspaper accounts of the period soon provided the money to send the Kensington Stone to Evanston, Illinois. There Prof. George O. Curme of Northwestern University examined it with great care, but he refused to verify its authenticity. If genuine, he pointed out, the stone would prove that Vikings not only had discovered America more than a century before Columbus but that they also had traveled a considerable distance inland in the second half of the fourteenth century.

Weeks after Curme expressed wonder and bewilderment, the big stone was shipped back to Minnesota. Undocumented tradition has it that once it was returned to his farm, Ohman dropped it at the door of his granary and, except for stepping on it, gave it no more attention.

Sometime after 1905, a native of Norway learned of the stone's existence and visited Douglas County to take a look at it. Hjalmar Rued Holand, earlier a student at the University of Wisconsin, had long toyed with the idea of putting together a book about early Norwegian explorations and settlements in North America. Ohman's stone possibly might give him valuable information, he reasoned. Once he saw it, he asked the owner to permit him to borrow it, and the farmer consented. Years later the scholar took it with him on a tour of Europe to publicize his new book, *Explorations in America before Columbus.*

The appearance of the scholarly book triggered a wave of interest that eventually turned into denunciation during the next few decades. At the University of Illinois, Prof. George T. Flom concluded that the characters on the Kensington Stone were "essentially modern." At the University of Chicago, Prof. Chester N. Gould went a step farther. He said that the message found in Minnesota had been inscribed by someone who was skilled in the use of mallet and chisel but who knew little or nothing about early Norse writings. Scandinavian-language books, of which a number were readily available, had provided the writer-on-stone with the symbols he used, according to Gould.

At the Minnesota Historical Society, members of a special five-member committee spent months studying the inscription and consulting language specialists. In opposition to the current scholarly opinion, they labeled the stone as genuine. Without endorsing that verdict, scholars at the Smithsonian Institution agreed that the stone was of such tremendous interest that it should be seen by as many people as possible. As a result, it lay under glass in Washington for much of 1948. Awed visitors were told that though its origin and message remained controversial, it was perhaps "the most important archaeological object ever discovered on our continent."

As part of the celebration of Minnesota's centennial as a territory, in 1949 it was sent to Saint Paul, where on March 3 it was dramatically unveiled by Gov. Luther Youngdahl. After spending half a year on exhibition in the capital, it was returned to Douglas County. There it became the showpiece of a museum, where it may be viewed today at a location close to the intersection of Interstate 94 and Minnesota 27, about 125 miles from the North Dakota border. In 1951 the Kiwanis Club of Kensington spearheaded a fund drive to erect a huge replica of Ohman's discovery at the edge of what many residents of the region had begun to call "the birthplace of America."

Possibly influenced by midcentury verdicts, a majority of

Symbols, mostly of the kind known as runes, must have required days or weeks to chisel into the soft stone on whose surface they appear.

today's experts agree that the Kensington Stone is one of the most clever—and baffling—hoaxes of all time. Nevertheless it is generally accepted that sailors from northern Europe really did reach the New World long before 1492. Early Norwegians settled in Iceland about A.D. 870. From that outpost, Eric the Red established a colony in Greenland about 985. Then in 1002 his son, Leif Ericson, is believed to have found a region of moderate climate somewhere south of today's Iceland.

Called Vinland because of its abundant grapes, this Viking settlement has never been positively identified. It is believed to have been the target of a colonization attempt by Thorning Karlsefni, whose party was driven away by hostile Indians. The now-famous Vinland Map, thought to have been prepared by a monk about the middle of the fifteenth century, strongly supports the oral sagas recounting Viking exploration of Labrador, Newfoundland, and regions to the south. Relics found near Saint Lunaire in what is now Newfoundland indicate that a Scandinavian settlement may have existed as early as the year 1000.

General agreement that these powerful rovers of the sea actually crossed the North Atlantic from Europe more than a millennium ago does not prove that they penetrated as far inland as Minnesota to leave the Kensington Stone as a record of their visit. Half a century ago, specialists in language and in

A very early Viking ship is depicted on the seal of the city of Bergen, Norway. [NORWAY NATIONAL ARCHIVES]

antiquities found several reasons to say that they did not agree with the verdict of experts at the Smithsonian Institution.

For example, these specialists said the letters AVM at the end of the eighth line of the message were universally taken to be an abbreviation of an unwritten plea to the Holy Virgin. And it is nonsense to think that Viking explorers of the fourteenth century would have invoked the aid of the Virgin Mary, those scholars argued, because in that era, Catholicism had not yet reached Scandinavia.

They also argued that the use of today's system of counting years was not in vogue at the time the message on the Kensington Stone was supposed to have been inscribed. Other scholars insisted that symbols on the stone that signify *opdagelsefard*, meaning "voyage of discovery," form a Norse word that had not entered the language in 1362.

Yet other persons with impeccable academic credentials have challenged these objections. They point to recently discovered ancient documents revealing that Catholicism was flourishing in some parts of Scandinavia many generations earlier than previously thought. This being the case, the AVM of the Kensington Stone is seen as a natural and spontaneous expression of piety.

Other scholars now insist that our system of numbering years was in use at least as early as the Middle Ages. Because Vikings were notoriously prone to raid and to plunder sites far distant from their own land, it is within the realm of possibility that some of them learned this method of notation and adopted it.

As for *opdagelsefard*, which has been called "the most controversial word in the entire message," some specialists now point out that it could have been in fairly wide oral use long before it appeared in documents written on parchment.

In the light of these and other findings, the controversy over the Kensington Stone has been revived and is today very much alive. At least one inquirer into the riddle of the stone's message, Orval Friedrich, proclaimed in 1986, "We can confidently say that the authenticity of the Kensington Runestone has been established; the battle is essentially in the past." Users of the Internet will find long and detailed discussions of every aspect of the stone's discovery and its message at www.sound.net~billhoyt/kenfaq.htm and other Websites listed there.

The Kensington Stone remains a center of controversy and of mystery. There's little evidence to support the contention that Ohman himself chiseled the characters into the slab, buried it for years, and then claimed to have found it by accident. This theory loses most of its significance when it is realized that he never tried to make money or to gain publicity from his discovery.

Regardless of when those enigmatic symbols were put into glacier-scarred rock, one aspect of the riddle is beyond dispute. Either a semiliterate Viking did the work or an unknown person later put a great deal of time and effort into mastering the shapes of runes and assembling 219 of them to form a message that, once inscribed, was tossed aside.

Today Olaf Ohman's find is on permanent exhibition seven days a week at the Runestone Museum: $1.00.

The Runestone Museum is at 206 Broadway Avenue in Kensington. Telephone: 612-763-3160. According to the American Automobile Association's North Central Tour Book, visitors should plan to spend at least an hour touring the place where the most fiercely debated piece of stone ever found in North America is housed.

4
George Catlin
Awed Onlooker

Nothing in his experience with members of numerous other Indian tribes had prepared an explorer from Pennsylvania for what he saw among the Mandans. These Plains Indians, who once dominated thousands of square miles of territory, were wary of white men who penetrated what is now northern Minnesota, the Dakotas, and regions to the south. However, because George Catlin painted a portrait that delighted one of their medicine men, the artist became the first outsider to witness the Mandans' most sacred ceremony, which lasted four full days.

Catlin's unforgettable account occupies thirty-four pages in the first volume of his book *Letters and Notes on the North American Indians.* Traveling by canoe in 1832 down a stream he believed to be the Missouri but which may actually have been the upper Mississippi, the easterner, who had earlier spent time with Assiniboins, Poncas, Sioux, Ricarees, and other tribesmen, was startled by the physical appearance of some Mandans. Their most imposing males and females had skin that to him "appeared almost to be white." This and the frequency of blue and gray eyes and "every shade and color of hair except auburn or red" persuaded Catlin to believe a tale he had heard while moving slowly into the northwest.

These pale-skinned Native Americans, he concluded, must surely be descendants of a long-vanished band of Welsh adventurers. The scientist Henry R. Schoolcraft, who had explored the region with the Cass expedition in the early 1820s and later became an Indian agent there, laughed when he heard of the artist's notion. Ridicule meant nothing to Catlin, however, as he had been mocked for years as an "Indian lover."

Though bestowed upon him in derision, the nickname was appropriate. For unknown reasons the man who was born in Wilkes-Barre, Pennsylvania, became totally enamored with Indians soon after Lewis Cass returned from his epic voyage to the northwest in 1822 or 1823. An artist who had made a decent living painting miniatures of subjects including Dolley Madison and Sam Houston, Catlin abruptly turned to Native Americans. For the rest of his life, he depicted their faces, their rites, and their daily activities as no other artist before or since has succeeded in doing.

It was his painting of the Mandan medicine man Old Bear, or Mah-To-He-Ha, that gained him a place as a spectator of the sacred *o-kee-pa* ceremony commemorating a great deluge in the long-distant past, much like the Noah story in Christian tradition.

Frequently Catlin was as fuzzy about geographical locations as he was credulous concerning tribal myths, so the precise spot where he was an awed onlooker cannot be identified. On the fourth and final day of *o-kee-pa*, the dance of the bull buffalo, or *bel-lohk-na-pick*, took place outside of the medicine lodge in which the white man was privileged to sit.

Catlin believed that an important goal of the unforgettable ritual was

for the purpose of conducting all the young men of the tribe, as they annually arrive to the age of manhood, through an ordeal of privation and torture, which, while it is supposed to harden their muscles and prepare them for extreme endurance, enables the chiefs, who are spectators to the scene, to decide upon their comparative bodily strength and ability to endure the extreme privations and sufferings that often fall to the lots of Indian warriors; and that they may decide who is the most hardy and best able to lead a war-party in case of extreme exigency. This part of the ceremony, as I have just witnessed it, is truly shocking to behold, and will almost stagger the belief of the world when they read of it. The scene is too terrible and too revolting to be seen or to be told, were it not an essential part of a whole, which will be new to the civilised [sic] world, and therefore worth their knowing.

George Catlin: photographed after launching his exhibition of paintings in London.

He described the sudden appearance of a naked and "unearthly looking creature" whose body was "painted jet black with charcoal and bear's grease," which brought the buffalo dance to an end. Once the eight male dancers with buffalo hair tied to their ankles ceased their rhythmic movements and incantations, the climactic *pohk-hong*, or torture ritual, was launched by two braves. One of them was armed with a scalping-knife while the other held splints in both of his hands.

Their bodies had been painted red, their hands and feet black. Each wore a mask that the artist believed was donned so that the initiates would be unable to recognize them after the bloody ceremony. Recalling the climactic ending later, Catlin wrote: "Thank God, it is over, that I have seen it, and am able to tell it to the world."

For five or six minutes, each initiate was repeatedly slashed below muscles, and a splint was inserted into every wound. Two cords lowered from an opening in the top of the big lodge were attached to the splints of a sufferer. He was then hauled up "until his body was just suspended from the ground." With blood spurting down his limbs, bystanders hung weapons and

Pennsylvania native Catlin at work on the portrait that brought him admission to sacred ceremonies of the Mandans.

sometimes a buffalo skull with horns attached upon the splints of the initiate. He was then hoisted up until his feet were raised six or eight feet off the ground.

Warriors whom Catlin characterized as "imps and demons" soon dashed forward. They turned their victim faster and faster until he became unconscious in ten or fifteen minutes and hung "with his tongue distended from his mouth." After having been lowered to the ground, a strong young male required six or eight minutes to begin to regain consciousness. With what little strength he still had, each such central figure of the ceremony crawled to a spot where a mature brave sat with a hatchet in his hand and a buffalo skull before him. After muttering a few words to the Great Spirit, the artist noted, a barely conscious initiate laid the little finger of his left hand on the buffalo skull—where a single blow of the hatchet severed it at the first joint.

No other artist matched Catlin in depicting the gruesome torture ceremony of the Mandan Indians.

The onlooker who had turned his back upon civilization in order to soak up all he could about Indian life and ways was surprised that "no bandages are applied to the fingers which have been amputated; nor is any attention whatever paid to the other wounds." Still burdened with weights fastened to him earlier, the youth who hopes to enter manhood is forced to run *eh-ke-na-ka-nah-pick*, or the last race. He cannot avoid fainting and is left where he falls until "by the aid of the great Spirit he at last reels and staggers to his wigwam."

During the ceremony, Mandans of every age—termed "the whole nation" by Catlin—watch while "raising the most piercing and violent yells and screams they can possibly produce." This ear-splitting confusion, he concluded, was designed "to drown the cries of the suffering ones, that no heart could even be touched with sympathy for them."

Small wonder that the native of Pennsylvania decided that Mandan males "outdo anything and everybody, and endure more than civilised man ever aspired to or ever thought of."

Despite his yearning to be fully accepted by these tribesmen, he admitted that his heart was sickened "with disgust for so abominable and ignorant a custom" as the annual observance of the *o-kee-he-de* ritual, which he concluded was dedicated to evil rather than to the Great Spirit.

Extensive drawings executed by the artist during the four-day ceremony have no exact counterparts. When exhibited in London's Egyptian Hall early in 1840, they created a sensation the likes of which had rarely gripped the largest city of the Western world.

Profits from his gallery, in which groups of transplanted Ojibways regularly performed, enabled Catlin to publish a volume of lithographs depicting hunting scenes and amusements among the Indians. Unlike his earlier volume, this one did not sell, and he was forced to give up the art collection to persons who held mortgages on it. Penniless, he returned to the United States in 1870 and made an unsuccessful attempt to sell a huge body of earlier sketches and paintings to the Smithsonian Institution.

The first white man to see and meticulously depict life among the Mandans died almost penniless. It took a century for him to gain recognition as one of America's great artists. Posthumous fame came, in part, from the belated realization that Catlin was among the first white men to visit and describe Minnesota's pipestone quarries, now a national monument.

At Fort Snelling during the summer of 1835, the artist learned that many Indians frequently came hundreds of miles to get some of the highly valued stone to make ceremonial pipes. According to the journal of an early settler, "the Sioux were very much incensed at the determination of Catlin to visit and inspect the pipestone quarries, a thing which no white man excepting one or two traders had been permitted to do."

Yet just four days after having arrived at Fort Snelling on August 17, the "Indian lover" set out on the long journey to what is now the extreme southwestern corner of Minnesota. He reached his objective on June 24 and ten days later sketched as the Sioux played a game in which a ball was prominent. On July 9 Catlin was fascinated by forty-five Chippewa who had come to get some of the red pipestone. Dressed in breechclouts, they performed a ceremonial dance and permitted him to see it from beginning to end. He found the region, the Sioux, and the visitors from afar so fascinating that he did not start back toward Fort Snelling until July 27.

Pipestone National Monument is off of U.S. 75 one mile north of the town of Pipestone. For information, call 507-825-5464.

5

Samuel Conner Pandolfo

Detroit on the Mississippi

Samuel Conner Pandolfo played his cards close to his vest. He never explained why he picked Saint Cloud as the site of the industrial empire he envisioned, although he often hinted that there was a good reason for his choice.

John Dominik, a staff member at Saint John's Abbey and University in Saint Cloud, thought he understood the fast-talking Pandolfo's reasoning. "Iron ore is abundant near this city," Dominik frequently pointed out, as though every native didn't know it. "What's more, a big timber belt is nearby, and in the World War I era lots of fine wood was needed for an operation such as Pandolfo planned—or said he planned."

We may never know Pandolfo's real reasons for choosing Saint Cloud for his empire-to-be, but we do know he had big plans. While at the peak of his career as a high-volume life insurance salesman, Pandolfo became fascinated with entrepreneurial success stories. One of them involved the work of Thomas Jeffrey in Kenosha, Wisconsin. An Englishman who emigrated to America in 1878 and built a bicycle manufacturing empire whose chief factory was in Chicago, Jeffrey turned to gasoline-propelled vehicles in the late nineteenth century. Transferring the trade name of his Rambler bicycles to gasoline-powered vehicles, Jeffrey built and marketed a two-seat runabout (with tiller steering) in 1902. It may have been the twin-cylinder twenty-five-horsepower Rambler of 1904—complete with wicker picnic baskets on both sides—that fired the imagination of Sam Pandolfo of Chicago.

Or perhaps it was another man's bold move that inspired Pandolfo. About the time Jeffrey was accumulating more

*Samuel Conner Pandolfo—
addressed as Sam by only a
handful of intimates.*
[STEARNS COUNTY
HISTORICAL SOCIETY]

money than he could count, Pandolfo learned that Henry Ford, an engineer for Detroit's Edison Illuminating Company, had quit his job, organized a manufacturing company, and made himself its president. Or it could have been another entrepreneur, James W. Packard, of the electric company that bore his name. A few years prior to Ford's entry into the auto world, Packard designed and built the first Packard motorcar.

Pandolfo was absolutely and totally fascinated with such stories, but he lost interest when his subjects failed. For example, he investigated another car maker, Alexander Winton, until he found that the car bearing Winton's name didn't make the grade. And he was surprised to learn that despite the success of his vehicles, former plumber David D. Buick failed to get rich. *Forget about Buick and Winton*, the salesman seems to have told himself. *Concentrate on Ford and Packard and other big winners.*

For whatever reason, Pandolfo chose Saint Cloud as the site of his "Detroit on the Mississippi" in 1917. By then the Chicago-based salesman who saw himself as a future leader of industry and finance had persuaded nearly twelve hundred people to buy stock in the not-yet-operative Pan Motor

Though Pan stock certificates were issued at $5 par, many of them brought $10 from eager investors throughout the nation. [STEARNS COUNTY HISTORICAL SOCIETY]

Company. He bought nearly fifty acres of prime land in his adopted city, began erecting a maze of buildings, and set out to hire the best men in the auto field. One of them, Edgard DeSmet, later moved to Willys and developed the basic design for the Jeep. Another was Victor Gavreau, who earlier had worked for Peugeot in France and who had close ties with then-famous race-car driver Louis Chevrolet. Gavreau designed and produced a motor for Pandolfo like no other in America. Extremely short, the four-cylinder device produced energy equivalent to that yielded by forty-five horses. Throughout the nation, auto enthusiasts who read rave notices about the soon-to-be marketed Pan motorcar vied with one another in singing its praises.

Meanwhile, the architect of the gigantic dream devoted much of his time and energy to the field he had already mastered—

Prospective purchasers cluster around a 1919 Pan. [STEARNS COUNTY HISTORICAL SOCIETY]

salesmanship. He recruited nearly five hundred experienced men and directed them to fan out and sell stock throughout the nation. Pandolfo assured his sales crew that they'd find plenty of buyers at the bargain-basement price of ten dollars a share. He was right; at the peak of the campaign, shares were being grabbed up at the rate of more than twelve hundred a day. Pandolfo succeeded in capitalizing the Pan Motor Company at five million dollars.

Somehow, though, car production never approached the sale of stock. By the time cars finally did begin to roll very slowly off the Saint Cloud assembly line, many impatient, would-be Pan purchasers had instead turned to Fords, Packards, Cadillacs, and other competing vehicles. Only five years after Pandolfo came to Minnesota, the third and last model of the Pan was produced, and the company's final auto was delivered to a purchaser.

Well before that, disillusioned stockholders and suspicious Minnesota state executives began charging that the promoter of Detroit on the Mississippi was either naive or a swindler. The maker of the Pan was charged with having used the mails to defraud. Since the ensuing lawsuit was a federal case, it was tried before Judge Kenesaw Mountain Landis, later the commissioner of professional baseball. Found guilty and sentenced to spend a decade in the federal prison at Leavenworth, Kansas, Pandolfo appealed all the way to the U.S. Supreme Court—with no luck.

Today he is compared with America's first great showman and is called "the Barnum of the Northwest." Those who reject that label are mostly of the opinion that the mammoth enterprise he planned and launched was grossly under-capitalized. "If he could have gotten his hands on fifty million instead of five," they reason, "chances are he would have given Detroit a run for its money."

It's unlikely that a universally accepted verdict about Pandolfo's short but spectacular career will ever be reached. There's a slim chance, however, that somewhere in a remote barn, made invisible by an old tarpaulin, a now-priceless Pan— perhaps a twin of the model that successfully climbed Pike's Peak in 1918—is sitting silently, waiting to be rediscovered.

6

Henry David Thoreau

In Search of Health

"I've tried every remedy I know," a Concord, Massachusetts, physician admitted. "Nothing has done you a bit of good.
You need a change of climate."

His patient showed no surprise at the verdict he received
after going through what then passed for today's annual physical examination.

"I've spent my entire life right here," he responded. "I think
you're right, but where should I go to find a climate that will
do more good than your medicines?"

"Europe. I've known several men and women about your
age who were having a hard time of it until they spent a few
months on the Continent. Every one of them came back invig-
orated and stronger."

"You well know that I can't afford to go to Europe; there's no
need even to think of it."

The physician pondered only briefly. "If Europe is out of the
question, you might try one of the Caribbean islands."

Shaking his head, Henry David Thoreau countered, "I know
some men who have been there and who came home com-
plaining about the muggy air. That wouldn't do me a bit of
good, since my lungs seem to be the source of my trouble."

"If Europe and the Caribbean are out, you still ought to travel
for your health. How about our brand-new thirty-second state?
I keep seeing newspaper stories that say Minnesota has the
most bracing air in the United States. You can go out there and
use the breathing exercises you've been trying here."

Within a month after that conversation, the man now revered
as "the sage of Walden Pond" made up his mind. "Minnesota

48

it is," he informed his friend Ellery Channing, who had tentatively agreed to go with him. Had the destination been Paris, Rome, and Berlin, Channing would have jumped at the chance to visit these famous cities. He was a lot less than enthusiastic, however, when he learned that Saint Paul—of which he had never heard—would probably be the largest city in which they would expect to spend a few weeks.

Sensing Channing's hemming and hawing as a way to avoid direct refusal, Thoreau turned to another friend, Harrison Blake of nearby Worchester. Blake was direct; he was not interested in going to a place near the upper end of the Mississippi River.

But Thoreau, the naturalist and writer, was now more determined than ever to go to Minnesota. Next he contacted the seventeen-year-old son of one of his longtime friends. Horace Mann had entered the small circle of Thoreau's intimates very early and had remained there after achieving fame as an educator. His son and namesake, an avid student of nature, had been exchanging letters with Thoreau since he was old enough to go into the field to observe small animals, birds, and plants. Invited to accompany the "old man" whom he revered, young Mann accepted instantly.

In May 1861 the two adventurers bought railroad tickets for the first leg of their journey. After stopping at Niagara Falls and Detroit, they reached Chicago ten days after leaving Massachusetts. Then they took a train to a river port, where they boarded a steamer and headed due north. Thoreau was surprised and delighted with what he found in the capital of the young state, and he was pleased to be labeled "an eminent botanist" by a Saint Paul newspaper. Mann, who never questioned a decision announced by his traveling companion, was pleased when told that they'd make the city their headquarters for several weeks. "From here, we can make a leisurely side trip or two," he was told.

It was the younger man who spotted an advertisement in the *Saint Paul Pioneer and Democrat*. Folding the paper so that the notice was prominent, he told Thoreau that they might enjoy the "Grand Pleasure Excursion to the Sioux Agency" that would begin on the afternoon of June 17. So many people were expected to go that the riverboat *Favorite* was scheduled to make the trip along with the *Frank Steele*.

This crayon portrait of Thoreau was completed seven years before he went to Minnesota in search of health. [CONCORD PUBLIC LIBRARY]

Keenly interested, the man who by posthumous publication would make little Walden Pond more famous than Minnesota's big lakes read part of the notice aloud: "Witness the ceremonies of the payment of nearly *five thousand Indians. . . .*"

"That refers to 'bounty money' promised under the treaties by which white men gain possession of Indian lands," Mann explained. Feeling near despair, Thoreau said nothing. Was it possible, he wondered, that his young friend did not know about his long interest in the "noble savages" who had been abused and cheated for many decades?

"The grand feature hereabouts is, of course, the Mississippi River," Thoreau confided to his notebook. He continued: "Too much can hardly be said of its grandeur and of the beauty of this portion of it. Saint Paul is a dozen miles below the Falls of Saint Anthony, or near the head of uninterrupted navigation on the main stream about 2000 miles from its mouth. There is not a 'rip' [current roughened by passing over an irregular bottom] below that, and the river is almost as wide in the upper as in the lower part of its course."

Once aboard the 160-foot steamer that would push its way

up the Minnesota River for nearly three hundred miles to Redwood in the Lower Sioux Agency, Thoreau became so excited that he reportedly wished he didn't have to go to sleep at night. Water fifteen feet deep—needed by the steamer—was often so close to shore that the vessel was "obliged to run into and break down at least 50 trees which overhung the water." This provided an exciting opportunity for the man who had come to Minnesota for the sake of his health. He wrote, "I could pluck almost any plant on the bank from the boat" so that it could be carefully examined.

He expressed astonishment that snags and "sawyers" (uprooted trees resting upright on the river bottom, with branches weaving and bobbing above the surface of the water) were abundant in the river. "The sound of the boat rumbling over one was the ordinary music," he wrote. It gave him a special thrill, he admitted, to travel in company with the governor of Minnesota, the superintendent of Indian affairs, a German band from Saint Paul—and a small cannon to fire salutes.

After a stop at Mendota, the excursion proceeded to heavily German New Ulm, about one hundred miles from their destination. There Thoreau watched with interest as stevedores rolled ashore a commodity for which settlers were inordinately grateful—one hundred barrels of salt. Having arrived at Redwood, he expressed surprise to find it "a mere locality, scarcely an Indian village," with buffalo reputedly feeding within twenty-five or thirty miles of the place.

On the second day of the conference in which "the most prominent chief, named Little Crow" was the spokesman for Native Americans, a cannon salute was fired after the payment had been made. "In the afternoon," Thoreau noted, "the half naked Indians performed a dance at the request of the Governor, for our amusement and their own benefit and then we took leave of them and of the official who had come to treat [parley, or bargain] with them."

In a letter to a friend he described himself as being "away in the far North-West, in search of health." Fighting what he described as "an incessant cough," he experienced little relief from it, but he tried to ignore it when absorbed with Minnesota's animals, plants, and Indians. After having spent most of three days among the Sioux on their reservation, he

This was the vintage and approximate size boat used in the grand excursion up the Minnesota River.

hedged a bit when asked whether he still considered these folk to be "noble."

After a full month of high adventure and crisp, clean air, Thoreau headed toward Milwaukee by way of Prairie du Chien. From that port he and Mann traveled to Goderich, Ontario, by steamer and there took a train to Toronto. Back home in Concord, he told friends that his most memorable single hour in Minnesota was spent on top of "a remarkable isolated bluff, some 450 feet high and half a mile long" that overlooked the river at Redwing.

Despite the laudatory language used by a Saint Paul editor in noting his arrival, Thoreau was not then widely known. Yet in Concord, he was respected despite being labeled as "eccentric." In addition to Horace Mann, his circle of intimates included Ralph Waldo Emerson, Bronson Alcott, and social reformer Margaret Fuller. Well-known friends at a distance included Horace Greeley, whose *New York Tribune* was the most widely circulated newspaper in the nation.

Thoreau's first book, published in an edition of 1,000 copies at his own expense, sold just 219 copies during five years. In spite of his financial failure as a writer, he continued to put into words his unique capacity to see extraordinary aspects of ordinary events and things. His reaction to the sight of little kittens merited just one vivid sentence:

Four little kittens just born; lay like stuffed skins of kittens in a heap, with pink feet; so flimsy and helpless, they lie, yet [still] blind, without any stiffness or ability to stand.

To his intimates he admitted that the journey to the Northwest failed in its chief objective, to improve his health. Within a year after his return, on May 6, 1862, he died, apparently of tuberculosis, then called consumption. A century passed before Thoreau, who was awed by the wonders of Minnesota and its people, was inducted into the Hall of Fame of Great Americans in New York City in 1960. By that time his lead in expressing moral indignation over social wrongs had influenced Gandhi and Martin Luther King Jr. in civil disobedience, and his love of nature was a beacon for conservationists.

7

Joseph L. Heywood

Bankers' Hero

Before he left for work, the bookkeeper at First National Bank in Northfield confessed to his wife his frustration with his job. "I like what I do," he said one morning in August 1876, "but the pay is miserably low, and there's no sign that it will get better. We're going to have to give up the notion of visiting the Centennial Exposition in Philadelphia."

Mrs. Heywood nodded wordlessly. For weeks she had known that her husband's dream of a trip to the East where they might get a glimpse of President U. S. Grant was out of the question.

"With Phillips out of the state," the bookkeeper reminded her as though she didn't remember, "I have to handle things that are really the job of the cashier. That means I may be late getting home tonight."

Just how late he would be on Thursday, September 7, he had no idea.

Around ten o'clock that morning, a powerfully built stranger sauntered into the frame building that housed the bank. Presenting a twenty-dollar bill, he requested change from the teller and carefully counted the four fives that were handed to him.

As soon as the fellow left, assistant bookkeeper F. J. Wilcox hurried to Heywood. "He's one of the riders who came into town this morning wearing those long linen dusters you see in sketches about Texas and Oklahoma," he confided. To Heywood, the man with a bushy black beard didn't look threatening, so he told Wilcox to get back to work. "Probably a cattle buyer staying at the hotel," he speculated.

Practically everyone in Northfield knew that three men

Bankers' hero Joseph Lee Heywood. [NORTHFIELD HISTORICAL SOCIETY]

riding powerful horses had cantered in from the direction of Cannon City fairly early. After eating a leisurely and hearty breakfast, they wandered around Bridge Square and leaned over a rail for perhaps half an hour to watch the current of the Cannon River. An hour later, another stranger appeared. Two more pairs of men wearing long dusters followed them into town at short intervals. This much of the day's events was substantiated by numerous witnesses. Soon, however, unexpected action came so fast that no two participants told precisely the same story.

One of the strangers pulled a revolver from under his duster and fired into the air, a shot later interpreted to have been a signal. With a comrade on each side, he then walked briskly into the bank. Seconds later each of the three bank employees had a gun at his head. After ordering that the cashier identify himself and being told that he was not in town, the leader of the men demanded, "Then who's in charge?"

Teller A. E. Bunker remained silent, and F. J. Wilcox said he was the *assistant* bookkeeper. As all eyes turned toward him, Heywood tried to go limp and slip to the floor. The gunman assigned to him, who had pulled out a two-bushel flour sack and was holding it with his left hand, was too alert to fall for that ploy, however. "You must be in charge," he snarled at Heywood. "Open the vault, and if you value your life, don't waste a second doing it."

An artist's conception of some of the fast and furious action in the streets of Northfield. [THE NORTHFIELD TRAGEDY, 1876]

"Can't," the bookkeeper gasped. "The vault has a time lock."

Heywood told the truth, but not the whole truth. As a pioneer national bank in the Northwest, First National's vault really did have a new and expensive time lock. Although the door was fully closed, meaning that the bolt had also been thrown, the combination dial had not been spun. Consequently, a pull on the handle of the door would throw open the vault, but the raiders did not know it.

Cursing, the bank robber who had charge of Heywood turned away from his captive and tried to scoop up loose silver. His revolver and his sack made him clumsy, however, so he picked up only some of the fifteen dollars that lay on the counter. He managed to thrust a bundle of what seemed to be bonds into his sack then put it aside and drew a huge knife that he held to Heywood's throat while demanding once more, "Open up!"

In the confusion, Heywood managed to break away and run toward the door, shouting a warning at the top of his voice. For that demonstration he was pistol-whipped by one of the robbers who paused in his movement toward the door. As the last member of the gang reached the threshold, he turned, took quick aim, and with a single shot killed Joseph L. Heywood.

Outside, citizens who realized what was taking place went into action at once. Hardware merchant Anselm Manning grabbed a rifle and began shooting. Youthful Henry Wheeler, a medical student at the University of Michigan who happened to be in town, did the same thing. Others fired from windows of the Dampier Hotel, emptying revolvers and shotguns in the general direction of the strangers. In turn, the robbers shot back wildly.

Two of the bank robbers—Clel Miller and Big Bill Stiles—lay dead in the streets. Nicholas Gustasfson, an immigrant who spoke no English, was caught in the crossfire and mortally wounded. Bob Younger had been hit but was able to ride. Already, angry citizens were throwing saddles on their mounts and preparing to organize a posse.

Despite the citizens' quick action, some of the bandits eluded capture for many days. During that time the posse eventually grew to more than five hundred men, one of whom was Gen. John Pope of Civil War fame.

Eventually identified, the James-Younger gang that invaded Northfield included some of the most famous outlaws of the West. Frank and Jesse James, along with Cole Younger and his brothers, had made their reputations as train robbers. Somehow both of the James brothers managed to escape capture after the Northfield robbery and made their way past the Minnesota state line before turning back toward the Southwest, where they had flourished for more than a decade.

Bodies of the gang members who were slain in the streets of Northfield were soon "resurrected" from shallow graves and shipped by Wheeler to his medical school, where cadavers were in short supply. The robbers were chased through Waterville and Mankat to Garden City, where the James brothers stole fresh horses and escaped to the Southwest. Their surviving

Jesse James as he probably appeared at the time of the Northfield raid. [THE POLICE GAZETTE]

comrades turned toward Lake Hanska, where a new gunfight erupted when they were trapped in Hanska Slough. Charlie Pitts was killed, and the three Younger brothers were soon captured on foot. Imprisoned in Faribault until put on trial, they entered guilty pleas to avoid execution under the laws of the period.

While in Stillwater Prison, Cole Younger was repeatedly asked to identify the man who shot Heywood. He steadfastly refused to talk, however, so the killer was never identified.

Lurid stories about the failed bank robbery appeared in newspapers throughout the nation. Editors of the *Boston Advertiser* informed readers that the cashier of a Minnesota bank "with a bowie knife at his throat and a pistol at his temple, returned a decisive 'No' to the demand of a gang of robbers that he should open the bank vault to be plundered." President John S. Prince of the Saint Paul Savings Bank and two colleagues mailed seven thousand copies of a circular to banks throughout the United States, its territories, and Canada. Dated September 20, 1876, it appealed for contributions to the Heywood Fund, launched by five thousand dollars sent to the bookkeeper's widow by the First National Bank of Northfield. Eventually Mrs. Heywood and her daughter, Lizzie May, received more than seventeen thousand dollars given in gratitude for the fortitude of their husband and father. Having paid with his life for his loyalty to the institution he served, Heywood was hailed as "the bankers' hero."

Soon forgotten outside the city in which he lived and died, the bookkeeper's memory was revived when leaders of the Northfield Jaycees reenacted "the great Minnesota bank raid" in 1948. The celebration was called "Defeat of Jesse James Days" because the name of that gang member had become famous through dime novels and silent motion pictures.

By 1976 the long-neglected First National Bank had been restored and had become the home of the local historical society. It served as the set for the reenacted drama in the centennial year of the James-Younger raid. Greatly expanded in scope, the festival now lasts five days and annually attracts up to one hundred thousand visitors. At the Northfield Chamber of Commerce, it is billed as the largest outdoor entertainment regularly staged in Minnesota.

Part 2
Unforeseen Consequences

John Charles Frémont, nationally revered as The Pathfinder.

8
John Charles Frémont
Jumping-Off Place

Lt. John Charles Frémont of the U.S. Topographical Corps knew he would have been trudging along a dead-end road of life were it not for an influential patron. As the illegitimate son of a young Virginia matron who had abandoned her aging husband to run off with a dashing young French dancing master, he never forgot that he had been boosted upward by an older friend.

U.S. Secretary of War Joel Poinsett, Frémont's longtime benefactor, made arrangements for him to go to the land of Indians and buffalo as a member of a party headed by French scientist Joseph Nicolas Nicollet. At age twenty-five Frémont had his eye on lovely Jessie Benton, U.S. Sen. Thomas Hart Benton's youngest daughter, who later eloped with him. He couldn't keep his gaze entirely fixed upon her, however, for he spent many days pouring over maps of the great Northwest, where he expected to venture soon.

More than twice Frémont's age, Nicollet seems to have left his native land in a bit of a huff after having been blackballed from membership in the Académie des Sciences. Deprived of the honor he most coveted, the French scientist came to New Orleans in 1832. Soon he realized that he still might make a name for himself, as an explorer.

Described by acquaintances as "one of the smoothest talkers you ever met," Nicollet went up the Mississippi River to Saint Louis. There he won the financial support of a fur-trading enterprise controlled by French interests when executives of Chouteau and Company bankrolled an expedition to what was then known simply as "the upper Mississippi."

During the winter of 1837, spent at Fort Snelling, Nicollet

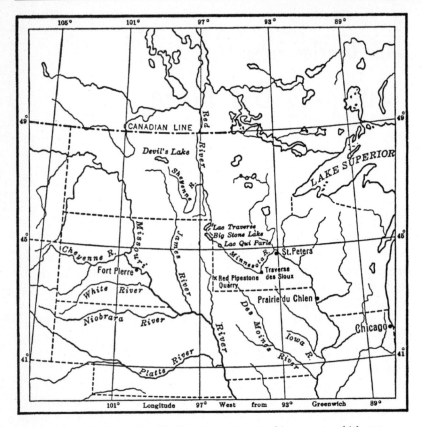

Prepared from findings of the Nicollet–Frémont party, this map—to which state borders were later added—was suprisingly accurate.

became enamored with Native Americans and was captivated by the notion of pinpointing what he always called "the one true source of the great Mississippi River."

Back in Saint Louis and unable to get additional funding, the scientist turned to the U.S. War Department. Secretary of War Poinsett agreed that more information was needed about the upper portion of the nation's greatest waterway. Nicollet also agreed with Poinsett's opinion that Zebulon Pike, Lewis and Clark, Stephen H. Long, Lewis Cass, and Henry R. Schoolcraft had "added immensely to our meager understanding of where the Mississippi arises." Convinced that the Northwest was rich in minerals, timber, and water power as well as furs, Poinsett wanted "a careful inventory of the entire region."

Nicollet's experience made him an ideal choice to lead a new expedition into the country destined to become Minnesota. What's more, Poinsett thought it would be logical to attach to Nicollet's group his youthful friend Frémont, the army officer with whom he had earlier been associated when both had lived in Charleston, South Carolina. Perhaps it might lead to the promotion of Frémont to first lieutenant, Poinsett speculated.

Long before he was officially added to the new exploration party, Frémont rejoiced at the great opportunity that was being given to him. He devoured everything he could find about the Northwest, aided greatly by the ease with which he read French, the native language of his father.

After spending some time in Baltimore, he and Nicollet proceeded to Saint Louis, where Frémont's U.S. Army status gave him entrée into a circle of officers stationed in the region. One of them, a captain of engineers, was especially gracious to the junior officer. "Given a chance," Frémont confided to his journal, "Robert E. Lee will someday make his mark."

After a German botanist was added to their party, the explorers proceeded by steamer to the mouth of the Saint Peter's River, now known as the Minnesota. Frémont was impressed by the American Fur Company executive close to his own age whom he met in the settlement of Saint Peter's, now Mendota. Henry Sibley, a man of prompt decisions and actions, presided over a virtual empire, for his trappers and hunters were spread out over present-day Minnesota, both Dakotas, and much of southern Manitoba.

Although he never admitted it to his fiancée Jessie Benton, during the time he spent at the fur depot or at nearby Fort Snelling, Frémont seems to have become smitten with a Sioux woman. Her name, meaning "beautiful day," was wonderfully appropriate, he confided to Sibley and to Nicollet.

Leaving her and what passed for civilization behind, Frémont and Nicollet set out for another fur trading post, Traverse des Sioux. To get there, they had to jolt through the wilderness in rough one-horse carts for an estimated 120 miles. From the trading post, they journeyed to the red pipestone quarry situated on a river bluff about three miles long.

Prized pipestone, Frémont discovered, occurred in a layer

Mrs. Jessie Benton Frémont polished—and may have embellished—her husband's rough notes made in the field.

seldom more than eighteen inches thick that was usually covered by twenty or more feet of relatively hard sandstone. Indians who came from afar sometimes spent many days digging before they reached their objective. Learning from a band of friendly Sioux that they expected to work long and hard to get just the right stone with which to carve a few pipes, Frémont persuaded them to delay their digging a few days until a cartload of supplies caught up with him.

Once the topographical engineer had kegs of black powder on hand, he used some of it to blow up the sandstone and lay bare a vein of the coveted pipestone before proceeding northward to still another fur depot at Lac Qui Parle. From this point, Frémont became the first American to thoroughly explore nearby sections of the Mankato River.

Nicollet had passed through this region on a prior visit laden with a sextant, a barometer, a thermometer, a chronometer, a pocket compass, a spy-glass, a powder-flash, and a device known as "an artificial horizon." All of this gear—the best scientific equipment of the period—had been used at a base on Schoolcraft Island in Lake Itasca.

This time, instead of spending a few hours there as earlier adventurers had done, the French scientist worked for three days and nights and succeeded in determining the latitude, longitude, and height above sea level. Then he carefully surveyed five creeks, one of which was noticeably larger than the others. "This creek," reported Nicollet, "is truly the infant Mississippi."

Being closely associated with the man credited with having finally pinpointed the source of the Mississippi River prepared Frémont to devote many years to exploration. His discoveries in the West did not come until later, however. Toward the latter part of his stay in Minnesota he returned to Fort Snelling. In company with other military men and a few civilians, he reveled in an opportunity to take part in "a royal hunting trip" in which Red Dog and other Sioux warriors led white men to the haunts of elk and deer.

Later admitting that he had been far from ready to turn his back upon Minnesota, Frémont returned to Saint Louis in December 1838. He brought with him a mass of rough notes and sketches, some of which would later be polished and refined by his wife, Jessie Benton Frémont. To Poinsett and other government officials, Frémont's reports about Minnesota and its riches constituted proof positive that the least-known portion of Thomas Jefferson's Louisiana Purchase was potentially the most valuable.

Long before this verdict was found to be accurate, Frémont became much better known than Poinsett, his benefactor. The confluence of the Mississippi and Minnesota Rivers was Frémont's jumping-off place for a life of high adventure and memorable achievements. Not long after having turned toward exploration, he was one of the first white men to set foot in such places as Westport (now Kansas City), the Great Salt Lake in present-day Utah, the Snake and Columbia Rivers, and the Sierra Nevada. His discoveries and adventures resulted in his nickname "the Pathfinder."

Soon after marrying Jessie and less than a decade after hunting deer and elk with the Sioux warriors near Fort Snelling, he played a major role in winning California for the United States. Sent to the U.S. Senate from California, John Charles Frémont was the first Republican nominee for the presidency. Among his hard-working supporters in the election of 1856 was a then-obscure Illinois lawyer named Abraham Lincoln.

9
Dred Scott
Political Pawn

Six feet, three inches in height, attorney Montgomery Blair towered above the aging Supreme Court justices to whom he bowed respectfully on the morning of February 11, 1856. As the attorney for a slave who was suing for his freedom on constitutional grounds, Blair knew that the trial was likely to have a major impact upon the election of 1856. Of far greater importance was its potential influence on the delicate national balancing act between states that permitted slavery and states that did not.

His client is believed to have been born around the turn of the century in Southampton County, Virginia. Following a widely observed custom, "little Sam" was given the surname of his owner, Peter Blow. During the War of 1812, Peter Blow had fought as a lieutenant of the militia and afterward took his family and slaves to a larger farm near Huntsville, Alabama.

Worn-out land that Peter didn't recognize as unsuitable for cotton farming proved unprofitable, so in near despair he and his entourage went to Saint Louis to operate a commercial rooming house. His slave Sam worked at domestic chores and was occasionally commended as "a very helpful boy."

Sam Blow watched the many river steamers leave the busy port, and at age nineteen slipped aboard one of them, believing himself to be on the way to freedom. However, when professional slave-catchers seized him, he was flogged before being returned to his master, and the captors claimed their reward. With every bone in his body aching and his back raw, the subdued young fellow abruptly changed his name to symbolize what then seemed to be the darkest period of his life. Thus he stepped into the pages of history as Dred Scott.

Dred Scott, aka Sam Blow, dressed for appearance before a Missouri Court.

Two years after Dred (aka Sam) was returned to Saint Louis, his master died and left a nearly penniless widow. She sent Dred to a public auction, hoping to get fifteen hundred dollars for him. Because he was small and apparently malnourished, when he stepped up on the auction block, the bidding stopped at five hundred dollars.

Dred's new owner, Dr. John Emerson, wanted a commission in the U.S. Army. When he heard of an opening for a post surgeon at desolate Fort Armstrong in Illinois, he asked influential men of his acquaintance to give him a letter of recommendation, and it is possible that Sen. Thomas Hart Benton opened the door for him. In February 1834 he began a nine-year career in uniform, taking Scott with him to Illinois.

Life at the remote army post proved so boring that within months Emerson launched a campaign for a transfer. His efforts produced no results, but in 1835 when the War Department closed Fort Armstrong, Emerson was ordered two hundred miles north into what was then the Wisconsin Territory.

Proceeding toward Fort Snelling, described as being located "at the headwaters [of navigation] of the Mississippi River," he naturally took his body servant with him. Possibly neither Emerson nor Scott knew that the Northwest Ordinance of 1787

Kentucky native Montgomery Blair sensed a chance to win national fame as Scott's attorney.

outlawed slavery in this region that later became Minnesota. Had Scott been aware of the law and been able to find an attorney to represent him, he could have sued for his freedom as soon as he set foot inside Fort Snelling.

Maj. Lawrence Taliaferro, operating from a nearby Indian agency, became acquainted with Scott and developed a great liking for him. When he returned from a trip to Virginia, Taliaferro brought with him Harriet Robinson, a slave about fifteen years old. When she was offered to Scott as his wife, he eagerly accepted, and ownership of Harriet was transferred to Emerson. Contemporary documents suggest that the bridegroom, more than twice the age of Harriet, somehow managed to have a marriage ceremony performed despite the fact that slaves rarely entered into a legal union.

Dr. Emerson constantly complained about "the unbearable winters" at his post and finally badgered his superiors into sending him back to Saint Louis. His departure from Fort Snelling was so abrupt that he left most of his personal belongings behind, but he took Dred and Harriet along. Upon their arrival at Jefferson Barracks, new orders awaited Dr. Emerson, and they could not even spend the night before starting toward Fort Jesup in Louisiana.

Proslavery Roger B. Taney, chief justice of the Supreme Court (1836–1864).

Less than a week in the swamps of Louisiana convinced the army surgeon that Minnesota winters weren't so bad after all. Ordered back to Fort Snelling late in 1838, after a brief stop in Saint Louis, the officer and his slaves boarded the steamer *Gypsy* for the slow trip northward. On the journey Harriet gave birth to a little girl, and because Eliza Scott was born in the United States north of the Missouri state line, she was automatically a free person.

After two more years at Fort Snelling, Emerson was sent to Florida. Because the Seminoles were at war there, Emerson left his wife of two years and his slaves in Saint Louis. While in Florida, the physician decided to give up his struggle for an army career. He moved to Davenport, Iowa, and hung out his shingle. He died there at age forty, leaving all his possessions to his widow. Returning to Saint Louis, Mrs. Emerson hired out her slaves for several years.

On April 6, 1846, Dred and Harriet Scott became plaintiffs in a case that went before a Missouri circuit court. Claiming to be "a free person because of involuntary residence in free territory," Scott asked for legal manumission and damages in the sum of ten dollars. Four years later a jury rendered a verdict in favor of the Scott family, but in 1852 the state supreme court overturned the decision. Scott filed suit again in 1854, this time in the federal district court of the state, where a negative verdict paved the way for a test before the Supreme Court.

Aspiring politician Montgomery Blair, an abolitionist who was eager both to win a major case and to enhance his own standing with voters, was crestfallen when an associate justice demanded and got a delay of one year. In the heated climate of diverging north-south opinion, with antislavery propaganda constantly showing up in print, Supreme Court Justice Samuel Nelson thought there should be a long cooling-off period. As a result, the trial was not resumed until a few days after pro-south Democrat James Buchanan of Pennsylvania was inaugurated as president of the United States in 1857.

Scott was never present at the hearing that involved his fate—and ultimately the fate of the two rivaling sections of the nation. Though he was illiterate, he may have known that abolition of slavery by Great Britain had made the United States the world's biggest slave market. Clearly, he was aware that persons who worked for or against him were less interested in him as a person than in the cause he symbolized.

The decision was handed down by Chief Justice Roger B. Taney on March 6, 1857. Seven of the nine justices agreed that Dred Scott must remain a slave. Furthermore, Taney said that as a slave Scott had no right to file future lawsuits in federal court regarding his bondage—or anything else.

Almost universally known as the Dred Scott decision, the verdict of the high court was a tremendous if temporary victory for southern forces. It helped to inflame abolitionists and triggered the famous Lincoln-Douglas debates, which propelled into the White House a Springfield, Illinois, lawyer whose previous top elected post had been a single term in Congress.

In Saint Louis, Scott never realized the long-range impact of the legal issue to which he was central. Even before the Supreme Court decided he was a slave, Widow Emerson had married an antislavery congressman and, probably due to his influence, sold the Scott family back to their original owners, the Blows, who soon emancipated them. Scott spent the remainder of his life as a porter at Barnum's Hotel in Saint Louis. He died of tuberculosis in 1858, three years before the outbreak of civil war that the Dred Scott Decision helped to precipitate.

10
Garrison Keillor
Lake Wobegon

Minnesota's most famous community is not found on the AAA state map, a situation that has bewildered many would-be tourists. Nevertheless, Garrison Keillor's fictional town of Lake Wobegon, its colorful inhabitants, and their favorite haunts are very real and dear to millions of Americans coast to coast.

The town originated in the mind of this talented Minnesotan who was born in 1942 in the town of Anoka on the Mississippi River. Except for a few years when Keillor took a break from the weekly radio program *Prairie Home Companion*, the hilarious escapades and touching moments of Lake Wobegon's residents, drolly reported by Keillor, have entertained, enthralled, and endeared themselves to listeners since 1974. Keillor put the first show together and led its performance in front of an audience of twelve in Saint Paul. Now packed auditoriums around the country delight in the cast's live broadcasts of *A Prairie Home Companion*, which always include the "news from Lake Wobegon," known throughout the land as "the little town that time forgot," where "the women are strong, the men are good-looking, and all the children are above average."

Very early in his life, the show's creator demonstrated a yen for applause. Gary Keillor (Garrison is the stage and pen name he's used since his teenage years) made his first foray into broadcasting with a live 6 A.M. radio show he somehow managed to put together featuring a "musician" playing wine glasses, a male singer, and, of course, Keillor. No one involved in this almost-amateur offering to the public could fail to be aware that Keillor was the dominant player. Not that he deliberately set out to upstage virtually everyone who ever performed

Garrison Keillor, long-time host of "A Prarie Home Companion," honed his skills by performing before live audiences. [MINNESOTA PUBLIC RADIO]

with him; by doing what came naturally, he simply couldn't help doing so.

A seasoned performer before he was thirty, Keillor joined Minnesota Public Radio in 1969 while he was a student at the University of Minnesota. He has been there ever since, "with a few years off here and there for good behavior," the network's Website boasts. The smiling man behind "the best-known voice in Minnesota" readily identifies the source of his inspiration for *A Prairie Home Companion*. While preparing an article on Nashville's Grand Ole Opry for *New Yorker* magazine, Keillor came up with the idea of a Minnesota version of the show. Keillor's live variety program, whose name was inspired by the Prairie Home Cemetery in Moorhead, would feature an appealing mix of music, stories, comedy, and "news" from the fictitious Lake Wobegon. Bill Kling, founder and long-time president of Minnesota Public Radio, didn't voice an immediate objection to the idea when Keillor approached him. As a result, says Lake Wobegon's creator, he immediately persuaded Kling that he—Keillor—"would be the perfect host for the show."

Right away, listeners to Minnesota Public Radio not only

A 1977 broadcast from Worthington, Minnesota, featured Keillor (third from right) with Judy Larson, Bill Hinkley, Bob Douglas, and Rudy Darling. [MINNESOTA PUBLIC RADIO]

listened to *A Prairie Home Companion*, they responded with enthusiasm at every opportunity. Letters of praise for the music and the monologues sometimes included pictures of his correspondents. Other letters offered advice and critiques. When Keillor devotees at the University of North Dakota heard a grammatical goof in a program, they rushed to the post office to register their surprise that such a thing could have happened. After another broadcast during which the writer/performer/singer had casually remarked that he missed the unique aroma of warm cow manure, a delighted listener promptly shipped him a big can of the stuff.

Launched in almost impromptu fashion and long produced on a shoestring budget, *A Prairie Home Companion* has acquainted listeners throughout the nation with the cry of the loon, how it feels to view the wreckage of a noted musician's plane largely buried in snow, and the solemn beauty of a Minnesota winter—the season that constitutes "the civilized time of the year, when weather establishes all schedules."

Since 1979, the show, complete with Powdermilk Biscuit

commercials, has been performed live before audiences all over the country and broadcast over National Public Radio. The early tours were confined to Minnesota, the Dakotas, Iowa, and Wisconsin. Later performances took place in Alaska and Hawaii. One was broadcast from the home of Mark Twain, and another went on the air from the home of Willa Cather.

Other settings have included San Diego's Sea World and the reading room of the New York Public Library. Small cities were not neglected, either. Two of the forty broadcasts selected for distribution in the twentieth anniversary collection of *A Prairie Home Companion* originated in Spartanburg, South Carolina. No matter where the live broadcasts originate, the show's focus is still Minnesota.

Though Keillor says he sometimes sits up until almost dawn, working on a script for the next performance, he never lets his scripted role in the program become too rigid to eliminate impromptu changes. Some of his many ad-libs are among his most frequently quoted lines, and no show is so strictly structured that there is no room for an appearance by someone who has not been announced.

On stage one day, Keillor has said, he was surprised suddenly to find standing close to him at the microphone

> a grizzled old man . . . , rheumy-eyed, swaying, incoherent, holding a harmonica, breathing into it. The audience actually clapped for him and people yelled, "Let him play!" Evidently they figured him for a great fallen talent.

Instead Keillor put his arm around the street dweller's shoulders and steered him away from the microphone. Eventually another member of the cast came on stage and led the fellow away.

After seven years of prairie reports, Keillor closed down the program, moved to New York, and later started a new program, *The American Radio Company*, which was performed before sold-out audiences. In 1993 the show's name once again became *A Prairie Home Companion*, and its base returned to Minnesota.

A Prairie Home Companion is broadcast Saturday evenings on *National Public Radio*.

11
Bison Herds
No Home on the Range

Artist George Catlin, though not a trained anthropologist, made priceless notes and sketches that tell us much of what we know about the customs of the Native Americans of the great Northwest. Among their most important annual ceremonies, wrote Catlin, was the *"bel-lohck-na-pick* [the bull dance]; to the strict observance of which they attribute the coming of buffaloes."

This ceremonial dance, he reported, was performed repeatedly during four days. On the first day, the fifteen-minute bull dance was performed once to each of the four cardinal points of the compass. On the second day, dancers whirled and gyrated twice toward the north, east, south, and west. On the third day, there were three dances at each point, and four on the fourth.

According to the artist-explorer, the bull dance was performed by eight carefully selected men. Each wore an entire buffalo skin thrown over his back—with the horns, hooves, and tail retained; a lock of buffalo hair was tied around each of the dancer's ankles. Assuming a position as nearly horizontal as possible, the dance could "imitate the actions of the buffalo, whilst they were looking out of its eyes as through a mask."

The beating of special drums enabled each participant to synchronize his movements with his companions. These drums were described by Catlin as "sacks containing three or four gallons of water." Fashioned from the skin of the buffalo's neck that was sewn together in the form of a large tortoise lying on its back, each sack had "a bunch of eagle's quills appended to it as a tail." Called *eeh-teeh-ka*, these sacks were objects of great veneration. While they were being beaten by sticks, accompanying sounds came from the shaking of *eeh-nah-dee*, or rattles, also made of buffalo skin and shaped much like gourds.

The enemies of the huge ox-like creatures also had roles in the bull dance. Two men with the skins of grizzly bears thrown over them continually growled and threatened to devour everything before them, wrote Catlin, the first white man to observe this elaborate ceremony. To appease the bears, women then brought out dishes of meat and put them before the men attired like the big predators.

Often those playing the part of grizzlies were foiled by "two men, whose bodies are painted black and their heads white, who are called bald eagles, who dart by the bears and grasp food from before them." The huge birds then were "chased by a hundred or more small boys, who are naked, with their bodies painted yellow and their heads white, whom they call *cabris*, or antelopes; who at length get the food away from the bears and devour it."

When Catlin tried to purchase some of the objects used in the bull dance, the Indians solemnly informed him that everything used in the dance was "*medicine*, and could not be sold for any consideration."

Like most of his contemporaries, the fascinated observer of the bull dance was of the mistaken belief that the buffalo (or more properly the bison) is native to North America. We now know that the big animal with the large head and neck and humped shoulders came to the New World long ago by way of the Bering Strait land bridge. Several types evolved, and at its peak the animal's population was so large that no reliable estimates have ever been made.

Like the Indians of the western plains, both the Sioux and the Chippewa of Minnesota based their cultures upon the animals. Whether a hunt yielded two thousand-pound bulls or females half that size, nothing was wasted. Buffalo meant food, clothing, shelter, tools made from bones, fuel from dung, and even glue from hoofs. Catlin asked questions when he saw a warrior pour fine black powder on top of his tobacco before lighting his pipe. This was pulverized buffalo dung, he learned, used to provide quick and very hot flames to ignite the tobacco.

To the artist, it seemed unbelievable that foods as different as pemmican and marrow fat—having "the appearance, and very

The bull dance is designed to insure plentiful buffalo. [GEORGE CATLIN]

nearly the flavour, of the richest yellow butter"—came from a single source. He once tried both of these staples, along with "a fine brace of buffalo ribs, delightfully roasted," before learning that buffalo had provided his entire meal. During this feast, he was especially impressed with a beautifully polished spoon, "black as jet," which his host eventually told him was made of the buffalo's horn.

Although buffalo were once numerous as far east as the Atlantic coast of North Carolina, by about 1825 they had disappeared from ranges east of the Mississippi River. The building of transcontinental railroads later fostered the killing of immense herds west of the river. When Catlin journeyed leisurely from "the mouth of the Ouisconsin [Wisconsin River] to the Fall of St. Anthony," he observed great stretches of tall grass north of Fort Snelling—forage to sustain hundreds of thousands of buffalo in the region drained by the upper Mississippi.

It is said that in Minnesota entire herds were slaughtered after the great Sioux uprising of 1862 for no reason except to deprive the Native Americans of necessities. Members of one

Indian hunters preparing for the kill.

punitive expedition recorded their satisfaction at having seized
and burned four hundred thousand pounds of dried buffalo
meat. Some officials of the federal government went on record
as holding that "Indians could best be forced to accept 'civilization' by exterminating the bison."

Already wiped out in the Land of Lakes long before they
ceased to roam the vast western plains in the 1880s, only a few
small herds of buffalo remained as Americans began to plan
for the advent of a new century. In 1894 Congress enacted legislation to protect the bison, whose numbers have increased
dramatically in modern times.

Nutritionists now know that Sioux and other tribesmen who
depended upon the animals as their most important source of
food were eating extremely well. Buffalo meat has only about
one-fourth as much fat as beef and now is recognized as a
"healthy meat choice for Americans." Private herds in western
states from which some animals are "harvested" yearly now
provide a substantial flow of steaks and roasts.

Like the aboriginal inhabitants of Minnesota, craftsmen today fashion jewelry and other objects from the horns and bones of the bison.

We will never return to the era in which millions of animals were slaughtered for their tongues only. Today a tanned hide that measures about six feet square sells for five hundred dollars, while the price of a winter robe made of the same hide approaches one thousand dollars. Although their ranges are extremely limited now and their numbers are pitifully small compared with the era in which George Catlin learned what they meant to the Indians, public interest in the huge grazing animals is increasing instead of diminishing. Internet documents that deal with bison (including sports teams that bear the name) will soon pass fifteen thousand in number—one Internet document for every three or four thousand animals that long sustained North America's earliest humans.

Reminders of the period in which bison roamed throughout the state still dot the map of Minnesota. Buffalo River State Park in Clay County abuts U.S. 10. The river for which the park is named meanders toward what was once the Dakota Territory for nearly thirty miles before pouring into the Red River of the North. Buffalo Lake and Buffalo lie a short drive north-northwest of Minneapolis, and a second, slightly smaller, Buffalo Lake is southeast of Mankato. Barring radical changes in place names, the big animal now never seen there in the wild will always be remembered in the Land of Lakes.

12
Billy Graham

Fate or Providence?

D_r. William Bell Riley, age eighty-six, was increasingly concerned about the future of the educational institution he had founded in 1902. The dean of Minneapolis pastors, educators, and evangelists knew he would not live many more years.

The longtime pastor of First Baptist Church wanted his Northwestern Schools to have the right president so his lifetime work would continue.

During the summer of 1947, Riley chose his successor, a North Carolina native he had met in Florida years earlier. "At my death will you take over Northwestern and run the schools as I did?" he asked him.

William Franklin Graham, known to relatives as Billy Frank, was so stunned that he was momentarily wordless. Nothing in his previous experience qualified him to serve as head of an institution of higher education that included a liberal arts college, a Bible school, and a theological seminary. He was totally absorbed with evangelistic crusades and his role in the Youth for Christ movement. Hence his initial reaction to Riley's unexpected demand was largely negative. His wife, Ruth, was emphatic that he turn down the offer, to concentrate his time and energy on mass evangelism.

After pondering for a while, Billy Graham reached what to him seemed to be a compromise that would be neither an outright no nor an unqualified yes. He agreed to become interim head of Northwestern Schools *if Dr. Riley should die within the next ten months.* What led him to specify this specific interval of time, he never publicly explained.

Shortly thereafter, on December 5, 1947, Riley died, and

twenty-nine-year-old Graham found himself a college president. Earlier, he had specified that if he were required to step into Riley's shoes, he would do so only on condition that he be permitted to continue to pursue his "primary goal in life." Hence he delegated most administrative details to Northwestern staff members T. W. Wilson and George M. Wilson, who were not related.

Graham was not inaugurated until June 1949, when the word *interim* was dropped from his title. From the beginning, he refused to accept a salary from the college and maintained his residence in Montreat, North Carolina. He conducted much of his administrative business via long-distance telephone calls to Minneapolis. Meanwhile, trustees launched a search for a permanent president.

During a 1950 crusade that Graham held in Portland, Oregon, many people who attended made contributions to help launch a radio program, *The Hour of Decision*. Far too involved in his evangelistic life work, Graham delegated the handling of these donations to Northwestern's business manager, George M. Wilson. Cautious and methodical, Wilson soon persuaded Graham that the funds should be channeled through a not-for-profit corporation, and the Billy Graham Evangelistic Association (BGEA) was formed.

In the fall of 1950, Wilson rented a room near what was then Northwestern College, which is now located in the Saint Paul suburb of Rossville. Soon he hired a secretary to handle mail and keep financial records. By the time the trustees of Northwestern found a new president early in 1952, BGEA was firmly established in Minneapolis and growing. Although Graham had not expected permanent ties with Minneapolis, it seemed desirable to keep this organization in the Land of Lakes, at least for the foreseeable future.

Growing up on a prosperous dairy farm near Charlotte, North Carolina, Graham was descended from Confederate soldiers, as was his wife. Billy's grandfather Crook carried a Union bullet in his leg until his death in 1910. His other grandfather, Ben Coffey, lost a leg and an eye during Pickett's Charge at Gettysburg. Both Billy and Ruth knew that Minnesota was 100 percent "Union country" during the Civil War, but this did not prevent these young adults from regarding the Land of Lakes and its Twin Cities with great affection.

Growing up, busy with morning and afternoon milking, Billy's universe was the South. At Sharon High School, he played baseball with enthusiasm but far too little skill to enable him to fulfill his dream of becoming a professional. With his parents he attended a small Associate Reformed Presbyterian church but had no life-directing religious experiences until age fifteen.

During the Great Depression, his father, while he was operating a mechanical saw, received a smashing blow on his head from a piece of flying wood. Surgeons did their best, but they admitted they didn't expect Frank Graham to live. His wife, who had recently become interested in a Bible class, refused to accept the medical verdict, as did Billy Frank. When they experienced "a miraculous recovery" within their own family, mother and son agreed that God had spoken directly to them.

In 1934, more than a year after this never-to-be-forgotten event, Charlotte businessmen put up a "tabernacle" for visiting evangelist Mordecai Ham. Initially not simply disinterested but positively antagonistic toward "meetings," sixteen-year-old Billy was persuaded by an older man to "give the preacher a try." After a stirring service, he was unable to sleep. With the full moon shining directly into his eyes, the boy had an experience that he found difficult to put into words. Later he described his unusual sensation that evening as "a kind of stirring in my breast." He also learned that pioneer Anglican evangelist John Wesley, too, had found words inadequate to convey his profound feelings, simply saying that his "heart was strangely warmed" during a quiet prayer meeting in London.

Before Ham's eleven-week stay in Charlotte came to an end, Billy had responded to an altar call and had totally committed himself. He said little about this change in the direction of his life to his friends and initially did not tell his parents. However, even a casual observer could see that something profound had happened to him; now his studies took precedence over baseball. That's why he did not protest when his devout mother made plans to send him to overtly religious Bob Jones College in Cleveland, Tennessee.

Later moved to Greenville, South Carolina, Bob Jones University took its name from the Methodist evangelist who founded it and who incorporated his own strict set of rules into the institution. Male and female students were forbidden

Billy Graham, America's most prominent evangelist of the Twentieth century. [BGEA]

to have physical contact of any sort; even "playing footsie under the table" at mealtime was taboo. Although Graham felt a strong urge to preach, he found the atmosphere of the Tennessee college too stifling. After a stay of only a few months, he transferred to the Florida Bible Institute near Tampa. There all students were expected to work, so Billy washed dishes, trimmed hedges, cut grass, and performed other chores. To him, a major plus for the institution was its role as host to vacationing evangelicals, most of whom gladly accepted opportunities to speak to students.

Billy was enthralled by sermons delivered there by Gypsy Smith. Homer Rodeheaver, who long served as song leader for Billy Sunday, held the attention of students when describing evangelist rallies at which thousands of eager seekers converged. Billy listened to Dr. William Bell Riley of Minneapolis castigate the low state of contemporary religion in America. In March 1938 he felt it impossible to resist any longer, so he "made a total surrender of his life in order to become a full-time ambassador for Jesus Christ."

Now with a clear-cut goal, he studied catalogs of numerous colleges, eager to get the best possible academic preparation

Northwestern College, Saint Paul, Minnesota. [PHOTO COURTESY OF NORTHWESTERN COLLEGE]

for his future career. After intensive soul-searching, he went to Wheaton College in Wheaton, Illinois, where he began to realize the significance of accreditation and the importance of unrelenting stress on academic excellence. By the time he learned what it meant really to study, he had made such an impression upon faculty members that some of them were involved in his 1941 selection as part-time pastor of Wheaton's United Gospel Tabernacle. Soon he became a full-time pastor in the Chicago suburb of Western Springs.

It was from Western Springs that Minneapolis entered his life. George M. Wilson of the city's First Baptist Church was an early enthusiast behind Youth for Christ, whose original meetings were held informally in New York City. When a Youth for Christ worker took the program to Chicago in 1944, Graham was chosen to deliver the opening-night sermon. Though obviously enthralled by the movement launched in Minnesota, his interest in it was diluted by an anticipated appointment as a second lieutenant in the U.S. Army. When it came, twenty-two-year-old Graham made plans to attend a training school for chaplains at Harvard University.

Providence once more intervened in his life. A severe case of mumps lasting for more than a month debilitated Billy, so he decided to give up his commission and to turn all of his energies into the Youth for Christ movement. As a field organizer, he visited Europe and Great Britain before going to Minneapolis for a 1945 rally. There one of his enthralled listeners was a man with whom he had become acquainted in Florida—Dr. William B. Riley.

Thus this chain of events answers a question posed by many an admirer of the evangelist: "Why is Minneapolis instead of Charlotte or Raleigh or Atlanta the world headquarters of your evangelistic association?"

After having been briefly headed by Frank Philipps of Portland—the source of gifts that required scrupulous handling—the BGEA was directed by George M. Wilson, who found time from his duties at Northwestern Schools to head the small office. Almost as soon as the BGEA was established, Graham suggested that a mailing list of potential supporters should be developed. Wilson strongly resisted; he had a low opinion of this widely used system.

Strongly influenced by the impact of the *Lutheran Hour* radio program, which was beamed to a national audience, Graham was approached about launching a radio program of his own. Initially cool to the idea, he was pursued by executives of a Chicago advertising firm. His message could be heard coast-to-coast for thirteen weeks at a cost of only ninety-two thousand dollars, they informed him.

To the man from North Carolina, that seemed to be a colossal sum, so he continued to balk. An offer of three weeks on the American Broadcasting Company's network for twenty-five thousand dollars came to him while he was conducting a campaign in Portland; the proposition was too tantalizing to be rejected out of hand. If the program he was inclined to call *The Hour of Decision* proved successful, he felt contributions might fund much of the cost of an additional ten weeks on the air.

Two Texans knew the evangelist was strongly interested in radio but doubtful about financing the proposed program. They made an unexpected offer of $1,000 each with which Graham could start his radio ministry. Still wary of making a

Billy Graham. [BGEA]

burdensome financial commitment, Graham left the issue in
the hands of his Portland listeners—and almighty God. After
the regular offering was collected for crusade expenses, he
described the radio challenge and invited interested persons to
make special gifts after the conclusion of the service. When the
single-night gifts were added to those from Texans, he had in
hand almost exactly the amount required for a trial run of three
weeks on the ABC radio network. Success of *The Hour of Decision* soon persuaded George Wilson not only to develop but
also to make systematic use of a mailing list.

    In doing so, he had ample names and addresses to feed into
it; weekly responses from *The Hour of Decision* reached twenty
thousand—then thirty thousand and finally forty thousand.

Later, when Graham moved into television, the BGEA became one of the largest handlers of mail in the nation. That meant that the BGEA was receiving large sums of money—most of it in the form of small contributions from tens of thousands of persons.

Evangelist Jonathan Edwards spearheaded New England's "great awakening" in 1734–35. His contemporary, George Whitefield, had extraordinary talent for persuading folk in the North to empty their pockets to support an orphanage he had founded in Savannah, Georgia. Later notables, Billy Sunday included, were accused of handling money carelessly. This "occupational hazard of the mass evangelist," plus frequent other violations of public trust, inspired a famous novel. Written by Minnesota native Sinclair Lewis, *Elmer Gantry* led great numbers of Americans to distrust all religionists who speak to or write for masses of persons. Fully aware that he "had to walk over mine fields and dodge booby traps," Graham and his BGEA have scrupulously avoided these pitfalls.

Affection of the common folk for Graham, whose Minneapolis offices are widely known to have handled large sums of money, has not been diminished by his image as "pastor to presidents." His involvement with our nation's top leaders began at least as early as 1951, when he helped persuade Dwight D. Eisenhower to seek the White House. A red Bible that he presented to the head of allied military operations in Europe was reputedly among Eisenhower's most treasured personal possessions.

Graham first visited the White House early in the administration of Lyndon B. Johnson, who with Lady Bird later attended the Houston crusade. Every successive chief executive has valued the evangelist as a confidant. Long before he became president, Jimmy Carter chaired a Billy Graham film crusade in rural Georgia. As governor of the state, Carter was instrumental in bringing the Tarheel to Atlanta for a 1973 crusade. Bill Clinton has followed the example of his predecessors and brought the evangelist to the White House as a friend and adviser.

During the decades of his ever-growing prominence, Graham has continued to maintain his residence in North Carolina. Did blind fate open the door through which he strode rather hastily in order to establish a tiny enterprise in the Land of Lakes . . . or was purposeful Providence at work?

There's no doubt about how the evangelist would answer that question!

Quietly dispensing big money on behalf of a wide range of religious and other service enterprises, the BGEA in Minneapolis has grown from a staff of one to a body of 399 workers. No other Minnesota enterprise guided at long distance by a world traveler continually on the move has a comparable story.

13

Henry Wadsworth Longfellow
Cultural Exchange

At age forty-seven, Henry Wadsworth Longfellow felt that he needed a new and difficult challenge. As the Smith Professor of Modern Languages at Harvard, he taught French, Spanish, and Italian and was familiar with several other languages. After seventeen years in the classroom it seemed to him that more and more students were after a degree but were not really interested in actually learning. To the consternation of his intimates, Longfellow announced that at the end of the 1854 term he planned to resign his prestigious academic post.

Months earlier the native of Portland, Maine, had become enamored with literature about American Indians. One of them, the central figure of largely mythical traditions, struck him as an especially heroic figure. Hiawatha, said to have been of miraculous birth, was credited with having guided fellow tribesmen in forming the powerful Iroquois League. What's more, legend had it that this wise warrior was the first man to plant and harvest Indian corn, or maize.

Hiawatha would be an ideal figure to cast at the center of an epic poem, Longfellow realized. Only recently having become fully acquainted with the Finnish epic *Kalevala*, he considered its unusual meter just right for use in lengthy unrhymed verse. That meant he had a key subject and a poetic style in mind before he made up his mind to quit the college classroom. All he needed was a store of suitable Indian names and a working knowledge of their customs.

Far to the west, a leisurely trip up the Mississippi River to see a pair of beautiful waterfalls had become all the rage among high-society people with time and money on their hands. As early as

Henry Wadsworth Longfellow. [H. B. HALL & SONS ENGRAVING]

1840, excursion boats were carrying sightseeing adventurers from both Dubuque, Iowa, and Saint Louis to the head of navigation on the great river. Upon arriving at Fort Snelling, persons making what artist George Catlin derided as "the fashionable tour" often went to sparsely settled Saint Anthony to spend a few days.

From that point, they toured the wide and spectacular Falls of Saint Anthony and the smaller but higher Minnehaha Falls nearby. The tourists were delighted to learn that in the Dakota language, *Minnehaha* meant "laughing water."

Some early visitors to the tip of what was to become Minnesota sent back to local newspapers lengthy accounts of what they had seen, and undoubtedly Longfellow read some of these reports. He also found exploration accounts written by Cass, Schoolcraft, and Frémont. He pored over the prints produced by artist George Catlin and read what scraps of Catlin's journals were then available.

Especially intrigued by what he learned about the famous red pipestone quarry, Longfellow revised his work plan and wrote "The Peace-Pipe" as the first of twenty-two cantos that make up *The Song of Hiawatha*. To his readers, he began by predicting they would want to know the origins of his stories, legends, and

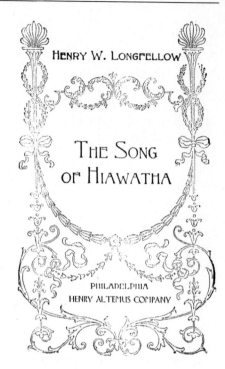

Title page of an early edition of the Indian epic that took America by storm.

HENRY W. LONGFELLOW

THE SONG OF HIAWATHA

PHILADELPHIA
HENRY ALTEMUS COMPANY

tradition "With the odors of the forest,/With the dew and damp of meadows,/With the curling smoke of wigwams."

All these came, he reported, "From the great lakes of the Northland,/From the land of the Ojibways,/From the land of the Dacotahs." He learned much from the lips of Nawadaha, "the musician, the sweet singer," he declared. But more came from the nests of birds, the lodges of beaver, the hoofprints of bison. Soaring into the thin air of Romantic poetry, Longfellow said that in addition to these sources of information, he learned from Chetowaik, the plover; Mahn, the loon; Wawa, the wild goose; Shuh-shuh-gah, the blue heron; and Mushkodasa, the grouse.

Lines of this sort are derided now, in the late-twentieth century. Longfellow, today's literary critics charge, had little or no firsthand knowledge of American Indians. He mangled some descriptions of the customs and manufactured Indian-sounding names if he failed to find a suitable one in the sparse literature from which he worked.

Objections of this kind were not voiced when the epic was

published in 1855. On the contrary, the American public went wild over the poetic account of the life and adventures of fictional Hiawatha. One publisher after another succeeded in getting permission to issue special editions of the epic, whose pages were often adorned with practically anything that had an American Indian look. In numerous cities, persons with established reputations as performing readers hired halls and sold tickets to those eager to hear *The Song of Hiawatha* read.

Along the upper Mississippi River, the impact of Longfellow's work was dramatic. It seemed that almost everyone who was anyone yearned to see Minnehaha Falls in person. As a result, Mrs. L. P. Hunt urged schoolchildren of the youthful state (admitted to the Union in 1858) to contribute one penny each for a sculptor to execute a statue of Hiawatha carrying his bride, Minnehaha, across a stream. Norwegian artist Jakob Fjelde made a plaster cast that was "an object of universal admiration" in the Minnesota building of the U.S. Centennial Exposition in Philadelphia in 1876.

Longfellow's lines elevated the red pipestone quarry to new interest and importance among Americans. Captivated by legends linked with the spot sacred to Indians, the poet began his epic as "Gitchie Manito the mighty,/He the Master of Life" called all the warring Indian nations together to wash off their war paint and bloodstains, to bury their warclubs, and dig red pipestone to fashion peace pipes.

From the Land of Lakes the easterner, who was the most widely read and admired of American poets at that time, had secured much of the best source material for his lengthy epic about Hiawatha. It was fitting that a reverse flow of this cultural exchange should take place. As a result, Minneapolis created Longfellow Gardens and successfully petitioned lawmakers to set aside money for something Minnesota did not then have—a state park. In 1885 a commission led by Charles Loring employed one of the nation's most prominent landscape artists to develop Minnehaha Park.

Today hosts of visitors who no longer study Longfellow in school come to the area to view the Minnehaha Falls with its statues of Hiawatha and Minnehaha as well as to shop at the world's largest mall. Thus the epic to which Minnesota contributed so heavily is still a significant factor in the character of the Twin Cities area.

14

George A. Hormel

Hard Work Pays Off!

One of German-American George A. Hormel's most vivid childhood memories stemmed from his family's grief as Abraham Lincoln's funeral train passed through his hometown of Toledo, Ohio, when he was five years old.

The boy's first job was as a carrier for the *Toledo Democrat*, a job that required him to get up at 4:00 A.M. and wait in line to get his newspapers until older carriers with more seniority had made their pickups. Young George stuck at his difficult, low-paying job for five years. His mother, who had immigrated to the United States when she was fourteen and had soon begun doing household work for the Millard Fillmore family, had taught him often that "hard work kills mighty few persons."

Had George not accepted that maxim as true, he wouldn't have taken his second job at age thirteen. In his father's tannery on Saint Clair Street, he became adept at pulling wool and tanning hides. The privilege of taking an occasional, refreshing swim in the huge vat where the hides were soaked constituted his only fringe benefit.

At age thirty-one, poised to take a risky career step, Hormel may have reflected on those first, grueling jobs—and those that had followed: He had done full-time construction work in Toldeo, laying lathes at two cents per square yard. He had worked in a meat market, earning ten dollars a month plus board. At age fourteen he had worked as a stevedore, or "dock-walloper." Next came long, hard hours in a lumber yard—a job that had brought him a jump in pay to fifty cents a day. Later he had earned sixty cents a day as assistant tender of machines in the Wabash Railroad shops.

George A. Hormel at age 20.
[HORMEL FOODS CORPORATION]

In Chicago at age fifteen, he had worked as a cashier in his Uncle Jay's meat market, spending his spare time at the cutting block, learning how to divide carcasses of hogs into their basic parts. Later he'd become a sausage maker and pork packer for Charles F. Unrath of Chicago, then he moved to Indianapolis, where he earned a weekly paycheck of $7.50 for packing pork tenderloins for shipment to Europe. At age nineteen he'd taken off for Kansas City, where the job market was so tight he had to wash dishes for his meals until Major J. N. Dubois hired him as a buyer for his hide-and-wool business at $75 a month. He ended up jobless when Dubois went out of business. Back in Chicago he worked his way up from common laborer for Oberne, Hosick, and Company, dealers in hides, tallow, and wool, to becoming one of the company's traveling buyers working out of Des Moines, Iowa.

From that base Hormel covered most of Iowa and the edge of Minnesota. Lying at the southern tip of the state (and the nothernmost town in Hormel's territory) was Austin, just over the Iowa border. Soon Hormel was spending the fourth weekend of every month there—and discovering it was the nicest place to work and live that he had ever encountered.

By 1910, a branch in St. Paul was using three delivery wagons; H. G. Cuneo stands in the middle. [HORMEL FOODS CORPORATION]

Writing to his mother on August 14, 1887, Hormel had confided that he had wanted to "quit the road" and go into business for himself. At the age of twenty-seven, he said, it was high time for him to begin making some long-range plans, but he was aware than his limited education could be a serious handicap. He had dropped out of school after the sixth grade.

After writing about his hopes to his mother, Hormel pulled into Austin one day and was aghast to learn that his best hide supplier's butcher shop had burned to the ground. The owner, Anton Friedrich, rebuilt—then changed his mind about continuing in the business and offered to rent the new shop to Hormel. He said if Hormel would go into partnership with his

The Austin complex as seen from the power plant in 1935. [HORMEL FOODS CORPORATION]

son, Albrecht, for sixty dollars a month he could use the new facilities for slaughtering and curing pork.

That's how George Hormel got his start in a Minnesota business that would eventually become worldwide in its impact. But Hormel's first goal had a more local focus: to make Friedrich & Hormel's butcher shop popular with the housewives of Austin and to boost their tiny slaughterhouse into becoming a full-fledged packing plant.

It only took a few months for the partners to realize that they had different goals; as a result, in 1891 an amicable separation left Friedrich with the meat market and Hormel with the fledgling packing plant. The name of Hormel's new business became "Geo. A. Hormel & Co."—despite the fact that its entire workforce consisted of Hormel and one employee, George Peterson, and it operated out of a tiny abandoned creamery half a mile from Main Street in Austin. Soon, though, they began to compete with Friedrich by operating Hormel's New

Cash Meat Market from a location well removed from the prime business section of Main Street.

By April 1898 the *Austin Daily Herald* reported that George Hormel had picked up so much business he had hired a stenographer to handle paperwork and there were now three male employees. However, as members of Company G of the state's national guard, the men were called into service for the Spanish-American War. On his last day at the plant, each member of the trio got a handshake, the promise that a job would be waiting upon his return, and a crisp, new ten-dollar bill. Despite the turnover in plant personnel, its owner decided it was time to put a full-time salesman on the road; a man named Sam Moe got the job.

By the time Jay Decker, Ben Hormel, and Harvey Chapin returned from service, their employer had arrived at another monumental decision. With sales moving upward, Hormel thought the time seemed right to put aside his well-worn meat cleaver and turn his full attention to management.

Having earlier reported the construction of a new smokehouse and storage unit at the Hormel facility, the *Austin Daily Herald* informed readers at year's end:

> The Hormel Company has been at work several months making great changes. Part of the buildings are already completed [at an estimated cost of forty thousand dollars] and are in use. Work on a big new refrigerator is under way. New pumps and engines have been put in. There is a fine flowing well of purest water, used for all cleaning and curing purposes. It is well worth a trip to the place to see what a big institution Austin possesses.

In the town whose population had edged just past five thousand, Hormel processed three times that many hogs in 1899. Ten years later, with the packing plant having processed more than thirty-two thousand hogs in the last twelve months and with assets of nearly $120,000 and liabilities of only $25,000, the business became a full-fledged Minnesota corporation with authorized capital of $250,000.

From the day he became a citizen of Austin and a partner of Friedrich, Hormel had fixed upon a single word as basic to the operation of a business: *expansion*. To plug along year after year at the same level might enable a business to survive, but in order to thrive he knew it had to grow. Growth could come only as a result of taking risks.

The meatpacker, who had learned the business from the ground up, then executed a maneuver that would become commonplace late in the twentieth century but was novel when he made the move in 1903. By means of a stock sale to John Morrell and Company of Ottumwa, Iowa, and the addition of three Morrell representatives to its board of directors, Geo. A. Hormel & Co. got an infusion of cash and entry into new markets. This joint venture lasted only four years, however, for in 1907 Hormel bought back the shares held by Morrell and again restructured the board of directors. Although the company's capital structure was doubled in 1906 just prior to terminating what amounted to a limited merger with Morrell, that wasn't enough to enable the fast-growing plant to keep up with its sales. By 1920 the value of capital stock had jumped to $4.2 million.

A limited part of that increase stemmed from the company's role in helping to feed the nation and its soldiers during World War I. Hormel went to Washington, D.C., to hear personally from food administrator Herbert Hoover the details of a system of controls for meatpackers. Government price controls proved to be a headache, but they were not nearly so great as the problems caused by the loss of 172 employees to military service.

When a gala "liberty picnic" was held in September 1918, nearly everyone present knew that Jay C. Hormel, George's son, had been the first Minnesotan to report for military service. He entered the service as a private, but within less than a year, Jay had become a first lieutenant whose recommendations concerning the handling of beef for shipment "over there" caused his superiors to bring him to Chicago's Quartermaster Depot.

Jay had demonstrated that he was endowed with many of the attributes that had brought success to his father. Clearly, he had the experience and the qualifications to serve as chief operating officer of a growing corporation. Less than a decade after Jay's participation in World War I, his father and mother built a new home in Bel Air, California. Soon after they moved west in 1926, they gave the Austin YWCA their home in that city as a gift. Today the brick residence at 208 Fourth Avenue NW, built in 1871, is on the National Register of Historic Places and is designated as the Hormel Historic Home.

Now global in scope, Hormel Foods Corporation is firmly entrenched in the Fortune 500 list of top U.S. business enterprises.

Part 3
Trailblazers

Fur magnate John Jacob Astor. [Engraving from Alonzo Chappel Painting]

15
John Jacob Astor
Long-Distance Merchant

Immigrant John Jacob Astor, who never lost his German accent and never learned to write fluently in English, reached America early in 1784. The ship on which he crossed the Atlantic entered Chesapeake Bay, and although it was in sight of land became so thoroughly icebound that its passengers were forced to remain onboard for more than sixty days. Astor ate little except salt beef and "biscuits" during this period, and he whiled away the time by becoming better acquainted with his fellow passengers. One of them, also a German, was making his second or third trip to the New World. While Astor, his funds depleted by the overlong stay onboard ship, ate a subsistence diet, he noticed that his new friend dined well at the captain's table.

His money, the man explained to his new twenty-year-old friend, represented "incredibly easy profits from the fur trade."

The son of a shiftless butcher, Astor had worked for a time in his brother's London shop where musical instruments were made and sold. In New York he worked for a baker and then became a peddler. Later he ran a music shop there. After less than two years in "the land of opportunity," he met and married a comparatively wealthy woman. In addition to a dowry of three hundred dollars, Sarah Todd brought Astor considerable experience in the buying and selling of furs. Soon she reawakened her husband's interest in the business that he had first heard about during that chance encounter in Chesapeake Bay. Turning his back upon flutes and violins, he set out to make a quick fortune as a fur trader.

England and Europe represented lucrative markets, especially for beaver skins, from which fashionable hats were made for

105

Frederick Remington's portrayal of a "mountain man"—hunter, trapper, and trader.

gentlemen. Even in Germany it was generally known that the vast forests and plains of North America supported immense numbers of fur-bearing animals. By buying at the source and selling three thousand miles to the east, Astor was sure he could get a good margin of profit—provided he could outwit long-established French and British companies.

The would-be fur trader couldn't have picked a more opportune time to enter the market. A 1794 treaty between the fledgling United States and the mother country led the British to evacuate dozens of frontier forts that also served as trading centers. This eliminated one of his prime competitors for the vast supply of North American furs, leaving Astor to deal chiefly with Canadian-based fur companies and French interests headquartered in Saint Louis.

By the time of Thomas Jefferson's Louisiana Purchase in 1803, Astor had already made a small fortune from a single shipload of furs he had sent to Canton, China, enabling the newcomer to soar into high financial circles. Soon employees of his American Fur Company were competing successfully with French-speaking *coureurs de bois* (French-Canadian trappers) for skins of the beaver, mink, otter, lynx, marten, deer, wolf, fox, bear, rabbit, muskrat, raccoon, and even opossum.

Without setting foot in the region that became Minnesota,

The Astor Library, about 1850.
[MAGAZINE OF AMERICAN
HISTORY]

Astor profited immensely from the skins of millions of animals that thrived along its many rivers and creeks. Even inferior skins were stripped of hair, and the felt thus produced was used to make relatively inexpensive hats.

As a political string-puller, Astor was as adept as he was in buying and selling furs. He successfully lobbied congressmen and senators to enact laws by which he squeezed out more and more of his business competitors. When the U.S. secretary of the treasury, Albert Gallatin, announced that the War of 1812 had left the nation in need of money, Astor came to the rescue of his adopted nation. Sometimes using borrowed money, the man whose fortune originated in the forests and streams of the Northwest bought great quantities of bonds at about 75 percent of their face value then paid for them in currency that had depreciated heavily.

Shrewd financial ploys and investment in Manhattan Island real estate caused Astor's fur-based fortune to multiply several times. When author Washington Irving heaped lavish praise upon him, the writer was accused, probably falsely, of having been paid to pay tribute to the fur trader. At Astor's death in 1848, few disputed the verdict of publisher James G. Bennett that Astor had become the wealthiest man in America—worth an estimated twenty million dollars. Of this vast sum, he left a pittance—forty thousand dollars—to establish a library bearing his name that is now part of the New York Public Library system.

16
The Lone Eagle

Twenty-Five-Thousand-Dollar Jackpot

Waving his press credentials, Edwin L. James of the *New York Times* made slow headway through the enormous crowd packed around Le Bourget Airport near Paris while estimating the size of the waiting crowds. Later he cabled his editors: "Twenty thousand still here; maybe twenty-five." Aviator Charles A. Lindbergh was already ninety minutes behind his announced schedule, but the crowd of spectators swelled as time passed. It was May 21, 1927, and many of the people had been standing there for five or six hours.

Earlier, rumors had spread through the throng that the former stunt flyer had been spotted over Valentia, Ireland. No one knew for sure if this report was accurate. Soon it was followed by word that a lone monoplane, flying straight east, had passed over Plymouth, England, at an altitude too great to distinguish its markings. Then a fresh report circulated that the man and the plane for which they had been waiting so long had passed over Cherbourg only a few minutes earlier.

James heard some members of the eager crowd voice negative reactions to this unscheduled news bulletin. "Too bad it isn't true," one gendarme commented. "He was a brave fellow even to make the attempt." Someone else confided to nearby companions, "They say he took along only the most primitive navigation instruments; he should have known better." A pessimist estimated that the American had one chance in a thousand of reaching his destination, but a nearby optimist

108

Congressman Charles Augustus Lindbergh of Minnesota, with son and namesake.

countered, "Bunk! He'll win the jackpot before the night is over; just wait and see."

The jackpot was a twenty-five-thousand-dollar prize offered to the aviator who made the first New York-to-Paris nonstop flight. New York hotel owner Raymond Orteig, an aviation enthusiast, had made the offer in 1919, but no one had yet won it.

Charles Augustus Lindbergh, who was brought up largely on a farm at Little Falls, Minnesota, was an optimist by temperament. Once questioned about this trait by reporters, he flashed his famous smile and explained, "My father was my teacher; if he hadn't been a real optimist, he'd never have remained a congressman from the Land of Lakes during my entire boyhood!"

Early in his adolescence, Lindy began managing the family farm that lay along the east bank of the Mississippi River. Soon he was called "a nut about airplanes" by schoolmates who didn't share his fascination with flight. After a couple of years at the University of Wisconsin, the Minnesota youth took a brief course in flying at Lincoln, Nebraska. In 1923 he made his first solo flight in a World War I Curtiss Jenny plane he bought for five hundred dollars. Unwilling to call upon his father for the cash needed to get extensive training, he became a flying cadet in the U.S. Air Service Reserve.

Considering himself to be about as good as most pilots who made their living by barnstorming, the young fellow from Little Falls signed up as a pilot for the U.S. Airmail Service and was assigned to a route that linked Chicago with Saint Louis.

Had the single engine of his Spirit of St. Louis failed during thirty-three strenuous hours, its pilot would have disappointed waiting crowds in Paris.

During the time he worked out of the Mississippi River port Lindy found financial backers who agreed to put up money for his attempt at the transatlantic flight.

Even before he left for France, Lindbergh set a coast-to-coast speed record, flying from San Diego, California, to Long Island, New York, in twenty-one hours and twenty minutes.

New York and Paris were not a great deal more distant from one another than the nation's west and east coasts, Lindbergh reasoned, and he had flown the continent "with gasoline to spare." That meant he could cross the Atlantic solo even if he encountered headwinds, he told his financial backers. His estimate proved to be accurate. When he touched down in Paris at 10:24 P.M., his tanks still held about fifteen gallons of gasoline.

Interviewed almost immediately after his thirty-three-and-a-half-hour flight by Carlyle MacDonald of the *New York Times*, Lindbergh described lack of sleep as his worst enemy on the history-making aerial voyage. He

Readers of the New York Times *were the first Americans to get on-the-spot news that Lindbergh had actually made it to his destination.*

admitted that because he sometimes "sort of nodded a little," he didn't always know just where he was when he woke up. Before his departure, he had stowed five sandwiches where he could easily reach them, but he forgot about hunger and ate only one sandwich and half of another.

"I made it," he told excited newspaper reporters, "but it wasn't all peaches and cream; I had to fight sleet and snow for maybe one-third of the flight. Sometimes this stuff was too low to fly under and too high to fly over—so I just had to plow through it."

His notes scribbled while pushing ahead with very poor visibility suggest that he sometimes climbed to ten thousand feet and at other times skimmed just ten feet over the ocean waves.

Heralded as "the Lone Eagle," the Minnesota-bred aviator received a cable from President Calvin Coolidge. Later the U.S. Congress presented him with the Medal of Honor; he was also awarded the Distinguished Flying Cross and the French Legion of Honor, and was made a colonel in the U.S. Air Reserve. Eventually he was given so many medals and honors that he ceased to count them.

Naturally, Lindbergh grinned that day when he accepted the $25,000 reward for the flight, but that shrank in significance

Raymond Orteig, a Frenchman who designated Paris as the terminus of the flight, wrote a check to Lindbergh on June 17, 1927.

when the *New York Times* paid him $250,000 for his account of the historic flight. Later he wrote a best-selling book titled *We* about his accomplishment. After receiving a ticker-tape parade in New York City, he toured seventy-five other American cities under the auspices of the Daniel Guggenheim Foundation for the Promotion of Aeronautics.

His later life was marred by tragedy when his infant son was kidnapped and murdered just six years after he became world famous. Public reaction to this crime led to the passage of "the Lindbergh Laws," which make interstate kidnapping a federal offense.

After the kidnapping the Lindberghs left the United States and lived abroad from 1935 to 1939. During this time Lindbergh worked with French scientist Alexis Carrel on a "mechanical heart," co-authoring the book *The Culture of Organs.* Although he was denounced prior to World War II for his isolationist views (he visited Hitler in Germany), when war started he served as a technical adviser to Allied aircraft manufacturers and then flew missions himself. Numerous military analysts insist that the antiwar aviator shot down at least one Japanese fighter plane.

In 1954 he won the Pulitzer Prize for his autobiography, *The Spirit of St. Louis.* Lindbergh died in 1974.

The fame of the aviator is so great that many tourists who

visit the Charles A. Lindbergh State Park, midway between the Twin Cities and Duluth, automatically assume that it commemorates his achievements. However, it was originally opened to honor the Lone Eagle's father, longtime Congressman Charles Augustus Lindbergh Sr. Adjacent to the park, the Charles A. Lindbergh House and Interpretive Center contains exhibits about three generations of Lindberghs, including the 1916 Saxon automobile that young Charles often drove. It is administered by the Minnesota Historical Society.

17
Richard W. Sears

Unconditionally Guaranteed

"Dick, you'd better leave well enough alone," a close friend cautioned. "These Saint Paul newspapers will take you to the cleaners in a hurry."

"Thanks," Richard W. Sears reputedly responded, "but I've made up my mind, and I'm going ahead with my advertising. The worst that could happen would be to lose the easy money I've made—and it may just pay off."

The year was 1886, and the twenty-three-year-old entrepreneur had just given up his job in order to concentrate on the R. W. Sears Watch Company. This was a radical career change for the Minneapolis and Saint Louis Railroad station agent who had started his job in North Branch, Minnesota, and later was transferred to North Redwood. Now working out of the railroad's offices in Saint Paul, he was opting to work full-time at the sideline business he had launched in North Redwood.

Located twenty minutes by buggy from the county seat of Redwood Falls, the North Redwood depot was empty and idle much of the time. Since business was so slow, railroad executives had yielded to young Sears's unusual request for special rates on anything shipped to him and by him. That way, he would have an edge on other merchants in Redwood Falls, because he would be able to sell at a little lower price. The enterprising station agent pointed out to his superiors that his use of the rail line would add a little to its traffic and hence to its revenue. Soon Sears was buying coal, lumber, and pelts and shipping them to distant buyers.

At that time it was a standard practice for wholesale merchants to send out goods on approval, shipping by train

Richard W. Sears, merchandise titan who made his Minnesota debut in so inconspicuous a fashion that his birth date is not known with certainty.
[DICTIONARY OF AMERICAN PORTRAITS]

merchandise that had not been ordered in hope that it would be accepted by the consignee.

In 1884 or 1885, a retail jeweler in Redwood Falls had refused a fairly large shipment sent to him this way by a watch company. When notified that the merchandise was ready to be returned, the watch manufacturer told the station agent that, to save the return-freight costs, he could have the entire lot of watches at half-price—twelve dollars per watch. Sears jumped at the opportunity and began dispatching messages up and down the line, offering watches at fourteen dollars each.

Sears's bargain timepieces sold so rapidly that he talked the manufacturer into another half-price shipment. When it arrived, he covered most of the floor of his office with packages holding four to ten watches, which he then dispatched to other station agents, offering them a "once-in-a-lifetime opportunity to go into business." It is said that during one six-month period so many watches were shipped from the small North Redwood depot that its station agent pocketed five thousand dollars.

Soon the railroad transferred Sears to Saint Paul. He left after a short time to go into full-time watch selling.

Sears, Roebuck, & Co. was born—not in a skyscraper, but in a little depot that consisted of the station agent's space plus storage rooms.

To his friends' surprise, his advertisements in local newspapers brought him so much business that he soon expanded into other cities and towns—soon selling to the general public as well as to railroad station agents. By 1887 he was so successful that he issued a thin pamphlet called "Catalogue #1." Its final page carried a then-novel announcement: "Every watch is warranted to be exactly as it is represented and every American movement is accompanied by a special six-year Certificate of Guarantee."

The concept of selling merchandise by mail was not new. The Chicago firm of Spiegel, May, and Stern had pioneered the practice. In New York City, Tiffany and Company jewelers had advertised the "availability of service by mail" as early as 1870 but did not make an aggressive move into this sales method. In 1884, R. H. Macy and Company distributed a mail-order catalog, and the following year the Larking Company was selling soap, coffee, tea, and spices by mail.

Thus in 1886 the Sears Watch Company was really a Johnny-come-lately in the mail-order business, but it went a giant step beyond the others. Dick Sears's guarantee was soon expanded to a specific, separate guarantee on the many appliances that he had begun listing.

Cover of "Catalogue No. 105,"
1897.

Realizing that Chicago was becoming the transportation hub of the nation's midsection, Sears moved there in order to ship merchandise at the lowest possible cost, and he soon diversified further. Many people wanted him to repair their watches, even though some of the timepieces had been bought elsewhere. On April 1, 1887, the *Chicago Daily News* ran a brief notice:

> Wanted—Watchmaker with references who can furnish his own tools. State age, experience, and salary required. Address T39, the *Daily News*.

As a result of the ad, Alvah C. Roebuck of Hammond, Indiana, quit his $3.50 per week job to join Sears.

By 1897 fast-growing Sears, Roebuck and Company was ready to issue Catalogue #104, whose size dwarfed the competing catalog of the older and better-financed Montgomery Ward and Company. The 1902 Sears, Roebuck catalog grouped the merchandise into forty separate "departments" and contained eleven hundred pages.

Addiction to alcohol seems to have been considered a nearly harmless tyrant; a trial box of 24 doses cost 50 cents—a $5 lot of them was billed as capable of curing "almost any case." A person who tried only a few doses, said the 1902 catalog, "will feel the craving for liquor disappearing; you will have a desire for food instead of rot gut."

Perusing the catalog provides a unique insight into the cost of living and daily lifestyle of middle-class Americans at the turn of the century. For example, in 1902, for just $10.45 plus freight a thrifty housewife could buy a drop-head sewing machine that was guaranteed for twenty years. Though he sold these sewing machines by the thousand, Sears preferred to ship a deluxe 150-pound Minnesota model that cost a whopping $23.20 and could be delivered to Charleston, West Virginia, by first-class freight for less than one dollar. One of his best pianos cost a whopping $98.50, but to help compensate for the high price, Sears guaranteed the instrument for "fully one-quarter of a century from date of purchase."

Many kinds of patent medicines, including some that offered a sure cure for the tobacco habit, were ordered in great quantities. Extravagant claims that embellished many bottles and boxes were the manufacturer's—not the retail seller's. An immense copy of *G. & C. Merriam's Webster's Unabridged Dictionary*—bound in sheepskin, no less—was priced at $5.00, but "our Stradivarius model" fiddle could be had for just $1.95.

A run-of-the-mill corset sold for forty cents and was described as "equal to any retailed at 80 cents." But if milady wanted a top-grade corset "modeled after the finest French shapes and made with soft busts plus stays of unbreakable wire," it cost her

"Every piece and part" of this bike, including its tires, was covered by the usual Sears guarantee. Customers who reached a negative verdict after looking it over could "return it at our expense"—an extra cost to the seller of 82 cents if returned from Bradford, Vermont.

(or her husband) seventy-five cents. Each sale of "A spotted dog overcoat for male or female, made from carefully selected black spotted pelts" brought the Minnesotan who was emerging as the nation's mail-order king fifteen dollars. Also available was "Lamb's Adjustable Animal Power Device," which had a treadmill designed to be powered by a family pet—a dog or a goat— that operated one of three separate devices selected by the turn of a switch: a dairy churn, a corn sheller, or a cream separator. The last of the three implements was especially popular among Minnesotans who had stopped planting their entire farms in grain and were experimenting with dairy cattle.

Although some of the merchandise might have been the butt of some rather coarse humor, by the time Minnesota's Charles Lindbergh flew from New York to Paris in 1927, more than fifteen million American households considered the frequent purchase of mail-order offerings an essential component of the good life.

Never turning his back upon his unconditional guarantee that had helped him shape the world's largest mail-order business, Richard Sears also won customers for years by shipping merchandise without prepayment. Purchasers inspected their orders at the nearest railroad depot before deciding whether to keep them or send them back. For decades the mail-order house tried to offer "anything and everything Americans need and use," including prefabricated houses—a few of which are still occupied today.

At his death in 1914, Sears's catalogs still offered an item that served as a fitting memorial commemorating the journey Sears had made from being the son of an impoverished Minnesota wagonmaker to becoming the world's largest retailer. Even in 1914, the era of Henry Ford's automobile, the catalog still carried a full-page illustration and glowing description of the covered wagon Richard Sears offered for sale.

18
Jay C. Hormel
SPAM

To his fellow residents in Austin, Minnesota, Jay C. Hormel, son of the founder of an international meatpacking corporation, seemed to be "just another ordinary boy except for his boundless energy." Far from being pampered by his wealthy parents, Jay began earning his own money very early. He bought grease from local housewives at two cents per pound then sold it for four cents. With a friend, he painted gasoline cans for the public at fifteen cents a can so the containers would meet local ordinances.

In 1927 at age thirty-five, he took over management of the company when his father retired and moved to California. Few CEOs of major corporations have assumed office at a worse time. It was during that time that economist Stuart Chase warned the business world, "We are all Alices in a Wonderland of conflicting claims, bright promises, fancy packages, soaring words, and almost impenetrable ignorance." On October 30, 1929, *Variety* used huge, bold type to warn readers, "WALL ST. LAYS AN EGG." The Great Depression had begun.

Ironically, the Depression brought about the product for which Hormel would become best known when President Franklin D. Roosevelt launched one of his programs designed to boost the American economy and feed the hungry. Under this program, the government purchased cattle at market price from farmers and then turned them over to meatpackers who were told to produce "a canned roast beef and gravy product for the nation's urban poor." This program lasted less than a year, but it inspired Jay Hormel to think of products that would appeal to the masses.

Jay C. Hormel as a student at Shattuck Acadmy, in Faribault.
[HORMEL FOODS CORPORATION]

He launched a test in which twenty-four ounces of canned Dinty Moore beef stew were offered for fifteen cents. The product got a huge boost when the comic-strip character Jiggs started mentioning it. Its success also was ensured by some innovational promotion ideas. In the difficult economic times, many corporate heads were cutting their advertising budgets, but Hormel took the opposite direction and enlarged his company's promotional activities. To promote Hormel chili con carne, which the company began packing in cans in 1935, the new product was publicized by a troupe of song-and-dance performers who became famous as the Hormel Chili Beaners. Next the twenty-member Hormel Drum and Bugle Corps hit numerous major cities and scored enough success to encourage the corporation's president to keep trying fresh ideas.

When he was ready to introduce a new product in which twelve ounces of spiced ham and shoulder meat were packed into a can, Jay Hormel played his cards cautiously. If the innovation should succeed, it would quickly attract competitors. In

Hormel Girls on parade at Eau Claire, Wisconsin. [HORMEL FOODS CORPORATION]

order to fend them off, he decided that his product must have a unique name. Therefore he offered a prize of one hundred dollars to the person who submitted the best name. Actor Kenneth Daigneau gleefully pocketed the prize money after having suggested that the ham-like product be called SPAM.

Spending in a fashion that some of his competitors considered lavish, Hormel used other advertising techniques. He moved into radio in California, and soon *Music with the Hormel Girls* was heard throughout the nation on Sunday evenings. A tour group of singing Hormel Girls grew so large that the entertainers began traveling from city to city in a caravan of thirty-five white Chevrolets. Although all of these experiments were successful, they gave no hint of what lay just ahead.

An advertisement based upon a
nationally syndicated comic
strip was "something new under
the sun" when it first appeared.
[HORMEL FOODS CORPORATION]

Americans not old enough to remember wartime rationing
cannot appreciate the way that millions of meat-hungry civilians reacted to SPAM during World War II. The product hit
Britain with such an impact that former British Prime Minister
Margaret Thatcher chose her words carefully when she later
described the Minnesota product as "a wartime delicacy." Production took a giant upward leap when military leaders made
it a semiofficial staple for use among fighting men. No one
knows how many remote outposts were named "Spamville" or
some equivalent by their occupants.

At war's end, Dwight Eisenhower took time to send to
Austin a letter of appreciation in which he told the packers of
SPAM that "I believe I can still officially forgive you your only
sin: sending us too much of it." Russian leader Nikita
Khrushchev later credited SPAM with turning the tide against

Russian stevedores are puzzled that SPAM is on their docks, but not in their dictionaries.
[HORMEL FOODS CORPORATION]

Hitler's Germany. "Without SPAM," he wrote candidly, "we wouldn't have been able to feed our army." His successor in office, Mikhail Gorbachev, came to Minnesota in 1990 and accepted a can of SPAM from Hormel's president.

Logic suggests that when the GIs came home from war and civilians were once more able to buy unrationed meat, SPAM should have had a decent burial. But nothing of the sort took place. By 1990, Americans were eating 228 cans of SPAM every minute of every hour of every day, and the meat product in a can was being manufactured in five foreign countries on three continents.

It took producers more than a generation to process and sell one billion cans of SPAM, but the two-billion mark was reached in the single decade that followed. By 1986 that number had doubled and was reportedly "increasing almost at the speed of light by comparison with 1937." With the SPAM trademark now registered throughout the world, its overseas sales may still be in their infancy as the product gains popularity in emerging Third World countries.

The product has been the butt of much humor. Because Jay C. Hormel got just what he wanted when he launched a competition to name the product, SPAM has become a household word, and today it's the subject of takeoffs and spoofs of nearly endless variety.

Yet SPAM's perennial popularity and ever-growing sales are not matters to laugh at. One of the best-known fast-food chains recently experimented with Spamburgers as substitutes for hamburgers, and boys and girls around the world delight in showing off their SPAM T-shirts and caps.

It makes a fellow wonder that if Jay Hormel knew back then what he knows today, what kind of prize would he have awarded for the winning name in his name-the-product contest?

Part 4

Record Makers and Pacesetters

An artist's portrait of Little Crow.

19

Little Crow

Uneasy Warrior

Abraham Lincoln's handwritten 1862 annual message to Congress fills twenty printed pages concerning the Civil War, fiscal matters, emancipation, and other national issues. Only one of the thirty-five states was explicitly mentioned; but half a printed page was devoted to it as the president told the lawmakers: "In the month of August last the Sioux Indians, in Minnesota, attacked the settlements in their vicinity with extreme ferocity, killing, indiscriminately, men, women, and children. It is estimated that at least eight hundred persons were killed by the Indians, and a large amount of property was destroyed. A large portion of [Minnesota's] territory has been depopulated. The people of that State manifest much anxiety for the removal of the tribes beyond the limits of the State."

Several factors had precipitated the bloodiest Indian massacre in American history. First was the departure from the state of thousands of able-bodied young white men, bound for the Civil War. Many Indians then were persuaded that the state, which had been admitted to the Union in 1858, didn't have the manpower to fight against both the Confederates and the tribesmen. Hunger also entered into the equation. A dry summer and the late arrival of the annual payment due from Washington meant that the majority of Sioux had produced little or no food of their own and had no money to buy it from traders. When a minor leader, Little Crow, appealed to trader Andrew J. Myrick for credit, the white man shook his head and snorted, "If your people are hungry, let them eat grass—or their own dung."

Long-simmering tribal frustration and anger were basic to

A Sioux massacre. [HARPER'S NEW MONTHLY MAGAZINE]

the start of a rampage without equal. Eleven years earlier the Sioux had ceded twenty-four million acres of land to the white man. That forced seven thousand Native Americans into a long but narrow two-million-acre reservation along the Minnesota River. In 1858 half of this land had been lost in another cession.

These Native Americans did not form tribes, strictly speaking. Rather, they were grouped into loosely organized bands, four of which flourished in Minnesota: the Sisetons, Wahpetons, Wahpekutes, and Mdewakantons. Lacking the pyramid of authority that prevailed among many Indians, the Sioux had no war chieftains. This meant that confusion reigned throughout the reservation after a minor squabble on August 17, 1862, led four young Wahpetons to kill five settlers living near Acton. Two of the bands wanted nothing to do with war, but the Mdewakantons feared reprisal for the murders, and many had long wanted an excuse to seek retribution.

In this emergency, chiefs of the four bands conferred and solemnly concluded that only one of their number had enough skill and prestige to lead them in all-out war against the settlers. Little Crow was reluctant to assume that role. "If we go to

As a member of Little Crow's war party, Cut Nose, is believed to have killed at least five men plus eighteen women.

war," he said, "the white men will descend upon us like swarms of grasshoppers." Despite strong misgivings, he eventually yielded to pressure and agreed to lead the warriors against "the thieves who have stolen our land" with the hope that the Wahpetons and Sisetons would join with them.

Few members of these bands became killers, and some of them risked their lives to save whites from death. Still, Little Crow could count on around nine hundred warriors once full mobilization of the two warring bands was achieved. Long before reaching the peak of their military power, the Sioux struck without warning at one isolated village after another.

On August 18 an estimated fifty settlers, most or all of whom had come from Germany, died at Milford Township. Fort Ridgely, the only nearby installation in which a few fighting men were stationed, became a mecca for refugees. Ten male settlers who headed for what they hoped would be safety were killed, and an equal number of women were taken captive. Since no survivors were left to tell what took place at the settlements that were completely wiped out, no

Merton Eastlick carried his young brother to safety on his back; later he became a member of a touring "panorama" group that presented the story of the Sioux insurrection to audiences in the East.

one ever knew how many died or were made captive that bloody first day.

On the second day of the insurrection, Little Crow wanted to send all of his warriors against Fort Ridgely, but about one hundred of them set out for New Ulm, a town that was obviously more vulnerable than the fort. To the surprise of the Sioux, the townsfolk were waiting for them with shotguns. During two days of fighting, nearly two hundred homes were burned, leaving just twenty-five standing, but the defenders suffered only sixty-six casualties.

When the attackers left, most of the town's survivors loaded 150 wagons with household gear and those too weak or old to walk, and headed for Mankato, thirty miles away. Some of their fellow citizens didn't consider that town to be safe, so they made for Saint Paul or Fort Ridgely. Both of these places, considered to be secure havens, were within one hundred miles of New Ulm.

At Sacred Heart, situated on the north bank of the Minnesota River, more than two dozen settlers were killed and scalped;

many women and children who survived the brief battle were seized and taken to Indian territory. Most of Lake Shetek's fifty residents fought bravely but were outnumbered by the Sioux. About half of the whites escaped; the rest were killed or captured.

Meanwhile, a courier raced from Fort Ridgely toward Fort Snelling with a desperate plea for help. Riding all night and frequently changing horses, William Sturgis covered about 125 miles in eighteen hours. In the capital, Gov. Alexander Ramsay hastily commissioned Henry H. Sibley a colonel and placed him in command of the state's militia. Initially small, by the middle of September Sibley's force numbered about sixteen hundred men eager to face half as many Sioux.

Delay enabled the defenders of Fort Ridgely to get reinforcements, so charges by warriors and a brief siege ended in the Indians' withdrawal. At Wood Lake, Sibley and his men had a decisive victory. Many of the defeated realized they would be hunted down if they returned to their camps, so they began a lengthy retreat toward the west. About two thousand Indians, many of whom were women and children, were rounded up and driven into stockades at Mankato.

When the brief but bloody war was over, twenty-three counties spread over more than one hundred square miles were devastated. Many settlers eventually returned to them, but others left the state and did not come back. Property damage was estimated to be around $2.8 million, an enormous sum at the time. An accurate count of the dead was never made; some Minnesotans believed the total to be around two thousand, but in the East the president's figure of eight hundred was accepted.

Knowing that he was certain to be condemned as a murderer if he returned home, Little Crow made an unsuccessful attempt to gain new allies among the western Sioux. Failing, he turned to Canada, where he hoped to receive aid from the British. When that failed he returned to Minnesota in 1863 with about two dozen followers and participated in the murder of at least thirty more whites.

While picking berries near Hutchinson, the minor chieftain who had been persuaded to become a war leader was shot and killed by a settler who didn't know the identity of the man he felled. True to Little Crow's early warning, the whites virtually wiped out the most vigorous group of Native Americans who once claimed all Minnesota as their domain.

20
Grasshoppers

Bane or Blessing?

Tradition has it that a wheat farmer in Jackson County—or maybe it was Cottonwood—was the first person in southeastern Minnesota to see what a horde of grasshoppers could do in half a day. Riding along the edges of his fields, the story goes, he came upon an acre of bare ground. Not a blade of wheat stood where it had waved luxuriantly just the previous day.

A strange buzzing sound, vaguely like the far-off noise heard as one approached a large sawmill, caused him to wonder what unearthly power had stripped him of one-seventh of his annual crop. By the time he realized that the vibrations were caused by the fluttering of millions of tiny wings, a vast swarm of grasshoppers had begun to strip another of his acres bare.

Numerous other counties, especially Pipestone and Rock, have their own stories of "the day the plague arrived." Some eyewitnesses are quoted as saying, "An enormous dark cloud blew in from the west very rapidly; when it came very near, an unearthly and ceaseless 'hum . . . hum . . . HUM' was heard from it."

The numerous firsthand accounts, seldom committed to notebooks or journals but transmitted orally for generations, date from May and June 1873. The "billions of millions of flying critters," as one person put it, were likened to the biblical plague that descended upon Egypt at the time of Moses. Today entomologists believe that the swarms of grasshoppers were the Rocky Mountain locusts.

Nearly a generation earlier, it was known that some unidentified insects had devastated a few isolated farms, but "the plague of '73" was much worse, especially since the farmers were still coping with the financial panic of 1870.

Believed to have flown from the distant West or to have been blown in by winds, most of the "hoppers" appeared during daylight hours. It took only a few days for settlers in stricken areas to learn that the winged army that seemed to be fifty miles wide and three times as long could eat practically anything. Wheat, oats, and rye seemed to be favorite foods, but when these crops had disappeared, the hungry insects turned to grass, trees, and even cloth. One housewife, desperate to save her garden, hurriedly threw sheets and rags over her plants as night approached. When she looked out the window the next morning, only a few ragged strips of cloth were scattered among the stumps in her garden. The grasshoppers had eaten all of her best sheets before turning to the plants she had tried to protect. Oral accounts, apparently trustworthy, say that in at least one instance ravenous insects ate the green paint off a cottage after having devoured every growing thing in sight.

Dispatches sent to the *Saint Paul Daily Pioneer* ranged from wails of despair to bewilderment. "Why did the hoppers ruin my fruit trees after all the wheat was gone but take off without doing much damage to my potato patch?" one farmer inquired.

No one had any answers for him or anyone else who was puzzled by the erratic behavior as well as the voracious appetite of the grasshoppers. It now appears probable that the 1873 infestation was triggered by a severe drought far to the west and perhaps to the south. When such conditions occur, grasshoppers are now known to make long migrations and sometimes to undergo physical changes that enable them to fly farther and faster.

At least thirteen counties were hit hard in 1873. In some of them, wheat production dropped by about one-third, and oats, barley, and corn suffered almost as much. Although a few struggling settlers were virtually wiped out, the loss to the state as a whole was minimal. The year's wheat crop dropped by only 2 percent, or a half-million bushels.

Accustomed to weather-related losses, many farmers simply shrugged their shoulders and went ahead with their preparations for the next year. Few of them realized that millions of grasshopper eggs had been buried just beneath the surface of the ground, awaiting the coming of spring. When those eggs

When huge piles of tar covered insects were set on fire, smoke could be seen for miles.

began to hatch, it was soon apparent that 1874 would be a much worse year than the previous one had been. This time, the wheat crop dropped more than five times as much as in the previous year. Many fields were stripped so bare that new immigrants found it hard to believe they had been carefully planted with the best seed.

This time the area of severe infestation was twice as large. Grasshoppers appeared in great numbers at points such as Mankato and Moorhead, which had not been affected in 1873. About one-fourth of the stricken counties were laid waste to such an extent that few farmers harvested more than one-tenth of a normal crop. Some settlers who had no crops at all mortgaged their farms to try to stay afloat, but hundreds of families gave up and moved out of the state. Their exodus was so significant that the population dipped in several previously fast-growing counties.

Down but not out, many a farmer set out to foil the insects during the following season. Ditches were dug around and

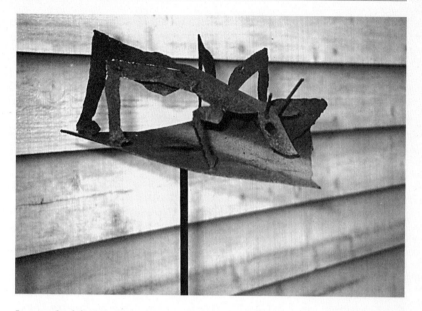

Just north of the Minnesota River, a Rienville County artist used sheet metal and a blowtorch to fashion a 'hopper who glares at passersby from its perch on an iron pole.

through numerous fields. Farm women accumulated all of the noise-making devices they could find, storing them in a central barn so the hoppers could be driven away at their first appearance. A few desperate folk bought smudge pots and when spring arrived began burning them around the clock. According to the *Saint Paul Daily Pioneer*, blacksmiths were kept busy all winter building "hopperdozers" designed to force insects onto big sheets of metal covered with hot tar or some other sticky substance.

These heavy, horse-drawn enlargements of the common fly paper brought fancy prices and actually did snare millions of grasshoppers. Covered with a flammable substance, the trapped grain-gobblers were dumped and scraped from the "pan" at the edges of fields and then set afire. Despite the thick black smoke and indescribable stench produced by such pyres, some families used them for weeks before confessing that they couldn't see that they had done a bit of good.

Control efforts and the weather allowed the damage to drop

a bit in 1875, but square miles of bare fields soared to a record high in 1876. Gov. John S. Pillsbury responded to desperate pleas for help by setting aside April 26, 1877, as a day of fasting and prayer for deliverance. He may have been influenced by editorials that appeared in some eastern newspapers. Activists on behalf of Native Americans alleged that Minnesota was being punished for having held the largest mass execution in the nation's history. Sioux who were hanged at Mankato, one editor alleged, were now "being avenged from the heavens by clouds of invaders so numerous that one hundred experienced hangmen cannot put an end to them."

Taking notice of Pillsbury's public gesture of piety, the American Tract Society issued a pamphlet declaring that after the day of prayer "a very unusual April snowstorm" caused immense numbers of grasshoppers to leave Minnesota. Apparently caught by sudden gusts of winds while moving from one farm to another, swarm after swarm seems to have been blown eastward—some traveling all the way to the Atlantic Ocean. That explanation for the departure of the insects before they could lay a full crop of eggs for the next season is buttressed by newspaper reports. One account described the decks of ocean-going vessels as becoming "as slippery as a Civil War ironclad strewn with the bodies of dead crewmen by reason of dead grasshoppers covering everything in sight to a depth of an inch or two." At Saint Cloud, a "grasshopper chapel" was built to commemorate "the deliverance that came from heaven."

Although grain farmers saw yields approach pre-grasshopper levels in 1877, many families had suffered so severely that they had already given up planting wheat and had imported a few good dairy cattle. After most of the grasshopper swarms had left the state, the trend toward diversification continued. By 1890 grain-growing regions that had earlier been laid bare by insects were dotted with so many barns that Minnesota had become a leading dairy state. The state's dairy products exhibited at the Pan-American Exposition of 1901 in Buffalo, New York, took many blue ribbons.

As a result, another nickname was briefly given to the state. Instead of the Land of Lakes, it was called the Bread and Butter State.

Grasshoppers have never been exterminated. At nearly every session the legislature passes one or more acts designed to deal with the insect and its impact. Yet there was a silver lining to the plague: Minnesota farming's diversification in general and the growth of its dairy industry in particular are the direct result of the grasshopper plague years that began in 1873. And one product of Minnesota's dairy industry now graces dinner tables throughout the United States and beyond: Land o' Lakes butter.

21
Judy Garland
Roar of the Crowd

Sold at auction, Jacqueline Kennedy's personal effects brought prices that astonished collectors and dealers. Many who expressed surprise seem to have failed to recall what happened in July 1988 when a pair of ruby slippers went under the hammer.

When the bidding stopped, the lucky purchaser of shoes worn by Dorothy in *The Wizard of Oz* wrote out a check for $165,000.

Had she been alive to watch the auction from the sidelines, Judy Garland would have reveled in it. After having achieved international fame, she talked with British reporters about some of her early childhood experiences. "I made my stage debut in my father's Minnesota theater at the close of 1924, well before my third birthday," she recalled. "My two older sisters sang first and got polite applause. After I sang 'Jingle Bells' for the fifth time and took a quick bow, the shouts and clapping of the audience sounded to me almost like Pokegama Falls. I'll never forget that evening—for that's when I became hopelessly addicted to the roar of the crowd."

There had been no shouts of joy when Mrs. Frank Gumm of Grand Rapids, Minnesota, confided to her husband that she was pregnant again. Frank looked as though he had been hit in the head with a lumberjack's poleax. His visible distress at the news and his repeated insistence that "two girls are enough in any family" troubled his wife so much that she reputedly jumped off tables and at least once rolled down a flight of stairs in a futile attempt to induce an abortion.

On June 10, 1922, at about 5:30 A.M., according to the *Grand*

Frank Gumm, father of Judy Garland, in Grand Rapids, Minnesota, in 1916.
[COURTESY JUDY GARLAND CHILDREN'S MUSEUM]

Rapids Herald-Review, the wife of a co-owner of the four-hundred-seat New Grand Theater gave birth to a daughter who was christened Frances Ethel. According to the newspaper, the stage of Frank Gumm's splendid establishment was large enough "to accommodate with ease a seven-piece orchestra." Nothing was said about the fact that after he became reconciled to enlarging his family, Gumm had confidently announced, "Ethel is expecting again; this time, we're going to have a boy and name him Frank."

Because she was seven years younger than her sister Mary Jane and five years younger than Virginia—both of whom were already performers on their father's stage—the child was nicknamed Baby. Because she was tiny and round and cuddly, the pet name seemed appropriate to those who knew the youngest of the Gumms. Some of them were on hand for her debut as a performer, when she sang at the annual style show presented by the Itasca Dry Goods Store a few months after her second birthday. Years after she wowed the movie-house crowd with her rendition of "Jingle Bells," she said that hearing that melody was "like taking a whole handful of wake-up pills at once!"

Her father, a mediocre performer who thought he might someday be a star, made a good living in Minnesota. He

Left to right—"Baby" (Judy), Frank, Ethel, Virginia, and Mary Jane, 1926.
[COUTESY JUDY GARLAND CHILDREN'S MUSEUM]

yearned, however, for larger opportunities than he found by
playing in Bemidji, Cohasset, Deer Park, Hibbing, and Coleraine in addition to Grand Rapids. It was Frank's restlessness
and ambition that took the family to the Los Angeles area just
before Baby's fourth birthday.

With his wife and three daughters, Gumm toured several
movie studios, where they caught glimpses of Lillian Gish and
Lon Chaney in action. Their greatest coup was scored at Metro-
Goldwyn-Mayer, where cowboy star Fred Thomson leaned
down from the saddle of Silver King and shook Frank's hand.
According to the *Grand Rapids Independent*, for which Frank

Judy Garland at the time of a triumphant appearance in London's famous Palladium.

wrote regularly, in an effort to see everything worth seeing in their new home, the entire family attended a religious meeting held by Aimee Semple McPherson. Baby fell asleep before they had been in their seats for twenty minutes.

By this time the parents were billing themselves as Jack and Virginia Lee—stressing that they also offered the services of the Three Little Lees "fully competent to render the very latest musical numbers and the Charleston, plus black face and impersonations if desired." More than a year earlier, Baby had wowed a Grand Rapids audience with her tiny and impish impersonation of Al Jolson. The Three Little Lees soon became the Gumm Sisters and for most of a decade earned enough to help keep the family financially afloat despite the fact that critics invariably panned Frank's performances.

Frances and her siblings were billed with George Jessel for a time, and he once blurted out to the radiant-looking little girl, "You're as pretty as a whole garland of flowers, young lady!" His comment triggered a change of surnames, so Frances

Garland soon became familiar to many Southern California theatergoers. She was nearly ready to go on stage one day when she stopped to listen to Hoagy Carmichael sing his famous "Judy." To her sisters, the girl exclaimed: "That's it! I'm going to be Judy from now on—Judy Garland, that is."

Songwriter Lew Brown heard Judy Garland perform and was so impressed that he urged her to try for a contract with a film studio. Frank Gumm, more than willing to act as his youngest daughter's manager, in 1935 worked out the details of a contract with MGM. This led to a bit part in the now-forgotten movie *Every Sunday*. Juvenile performers were popular during this period, but Judy didn't click immediately, although she had small parts in *Pigskin Parade, Listen, Darling*, and *Broadway Melody of 1938*, which was released in 1937 when she was fifteen.

Her career turned upward when she was teamed with Mickey Rooney in *Thoroughbreds Don't Cry*—a relationship that continued through *Love Finds Andy Hardy, Babes in Arms, Babes on Broadway*, and *Girl Crazy*. These films were box office successes, and Judy became an increasingly well-known performer several years from becoming an adult.

MGM executives searched for just the right vehicle to make the most of Judy's talents. They settled upon a musical version of *The Wizard of Oz*, long a staple in juvenile literature and the most popular of numerous Oz books by L. Frank Baum.

MGM couldn't have picked a less opportune season for release of an expensive venture. *Gone with the Wind* was the sensation of the movie world in 1939. Yet the public couldn't get enough of the film version of Baum's famous story about a wizard, an Emerald City, and a persistent little girl. Millions of moviegoers who were captivated by Judy's rendition of "Over the Rainbow" were delighted that the young actress was awarded a special Academy Award for her performance.

Having achieved stardom, Judy made a smooth transition into adult singing roles. She was featured in such films as the 1940 hit *Strike Up the Band* as well as *Meet Me in St. Louis* and *Easter Parade* in 1948, although by that time she was becoming increasingly dependent on prescription drugs. Alcohol and depression compounded her problems, and by 1954, when she gave an Oscar-nominated performance in *A Star Is Born*, she had already made at least one suicide attempt.

A brilliant torch singer as well as an actress, she died at age forty-seven of an overdose of sleeping pills in 1969 following a club engagement in London.

The family's spotlight-grabbing tradition lives on in Judy Garland's daughter Liza Minelli, who, like her mother, is a riveting performer. She, too, received an Oscar; hers was for best actress in *Cabaret* (1972).

22
Thomas Jefferson
Land Grabber

Thomas Jefferson has been called a Renaissance man because of his versatility. Our third president, who was almost six feet, three inches tall at a time when most men were much shorter, became skilled in a great many fields. Much more than head of the nation, he was also an inventor; he designed and built a two-faced clock that could be seen both inside and outside his mansion. He played the violin with considerable skill. He devised one of the earliest swivel chairs used in North America and designed a plow moldboard that won a gold medal in a French exposition. He was the first American to grow merino sheep, famous in Europe for their fine wool. He mastered botany, meteorology, and mechanical engineering. He became such an accomplished architect that he designed and built his magnificent Virginia home, Monticello, and planned the buildings of the University of Virginia.

Few biographers who have described the life and deeds of Jefferson acknowledge that many aristocrats of his day looked down their noses at him. "He's nothing but a carelessly dressed land-grabber," several wealthy Virginians agreed. "If we live long enough, we'll see him dead broke—owning so much land he can't afford to do anything with it."

That prediction, which surfaced well before Jefferson defeated John Adams of Massachusetts for the presidency in 1800, proved to be correct. Not until years afterward, however, did ordinary folk discover just how desperately the master of Monticello yearned for land—*lots* of land—in both his public and his private life.

While residing in what was then called the Executive Man-

Jefferson during his tenure as U.S. secretary of state, prior to the presidency. [CHARLES WILLSON PEALE, ABOUT 1791]

sion, Jefferson learned that Napoleon I was badly in need of money to finance his wars. The president notified the U.S. minister in Paris that he should make "discreet but diligent inquiries." Secrecy was important, because if other nations learned that French land in the New World was about to be sold, they might make competing offers for it. Diligent inquiries were essential because no one—not even Napoleon, and certainly not the president of the United States—had any idea how much land might be involved.

James Monroe was handpicked by Jefferson as a special envoy to France. He sailed on March 8, 1803, with instructions to buy New Orleans, and some additional land perhaps seventy-five thousand acres.

Having been authorized to offer Napoleon as much as $9 million, Monroe was sure he could get at least a little of what Jefferson wanted for the United States. He was taken aback on Easter Sunday when the French ruler notified him that all of that nation's land in North America was for sale. After days of haggling, Monroe and his colleague, Robert Livingston—who

James Monroe, authorized by Jefferson to buy land from Napoleon, initially regarded New Orleans as his chief target.

knew that they had 100 percent support from Jefferson—agreed to pay $15 million for a tract of land that was about half as large as all of Europe. To the undisguised delight of Thomas Jefferson, a formal agreement was signed on April 30, 1803.

When news of the secret deal leaked out, many prominent Americans were furious with the president. "The less of territory, the better," one of them wrote, charging, "By adding an unmeasured world beyond the Mississippi [to the U.S.], we rush like a comet into infinite space."

It took several years for average citizens to learn that the chief executive had acquired through the Louisiana Purchase about 533 million acres at a cost of just under three cents an acre. His land grab while serving as chief executive stretched all the way from the Gulf of Mexico to Canada. He acted without congressional approval and agreed to pay so much money that the United States had to borrow to cover its obligation. Had he not taken these rash steps in what critics denounced as "a most high-handed fashion," French might have been the dominant language of Minnesota today.

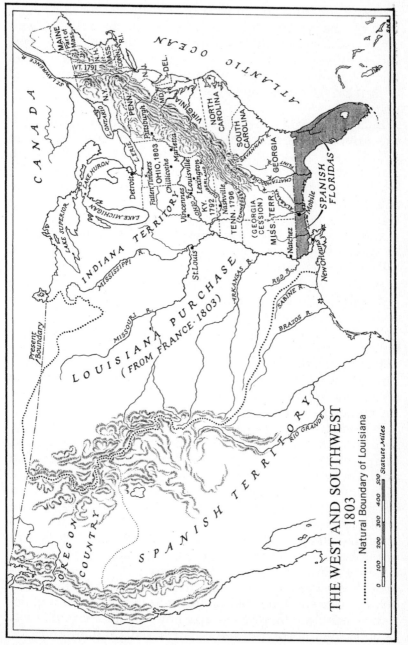

Regions that today make up the 48 contiguous United States, as they appeared after the Louisiana Purchase.

The president who acquired the Northwest for our nation never came within hundreds of miles of the Falls of Saint Anthony or the red pipestone quarry or the source of the Mississippi River. He was keenly interested in American Indian life, but he never saw the bull buffalo dance, a prairie dotted with what was then called "tepis," or a Sioux decked out to go to war.

In his personal life as well as his role as president, the chief executive who acquired Minnesota—along with most or all of Louisiana, Arkansas, Missouri, Iowa, North Dakota, South Dakota, Nebraska, Kansas, Oklahoma, New Mexico, Colorado, Wyoming, and Montana—was eager to get possession of as much land as possible. Anytime he learned that a large tract in his native state was to be sold, he submitted a bid without having seen the acreage. Since the Commonwealth of Virginia then included all of present-day West Virginia, his holdings eventually stretched for many miles to the west.

Unfortunately, his personal land speculation didn't turn out well for the man called Long Tom. Tobacco and cotton were eventually produced on some of the farmland he once held, but the land at the edge of the Allegheny Mountains never became productive.

The Louisiana Purchase, however, was a different story. The forests, furs, iron mines, and water power of Minnesota alone proved to be worth much more than a thousand times the money paid to Napoleon for the entire territory.

Personally holding uncounted thousands of acres of undeveloped land, by 1808 the man who masterminded the Louisiana Purchase was badly overextended and deeply in debt. On behalf of the United States, he didn't want to give up a single acre in Minnesota or anywhere else. Similarly, on his own behalf, he preferred "genteel poverty" to parting with any of his own holdings.

In this dilemma, the man who practically doubled the size of the United States in a single international deal turned to the Virginia legislature for help. Lawmakers were sympathetic but turned down his plea for a loan of eighty thousand dollars from the state. Desperate, he sought and got permission to offer his Monticello mansion for sale by public lottery. Tickets were printed, distributed, and offered for sale—but except for personal friends, few wanted to help the author of the Declaration of Independence by trying their luck.

Six months or so after his lottery plan fizzled, the man responsible for adding the unexplored Northwest to the United States died holding deeds to thousands of acres of what many then considered to be worthless land. Eventually Monticello went on the auction block as a result of Thomas Jefferson's eagerness to acquire more and more land for himself.

23
David Karpeles

Originals Only

Growing up in Duluth, David Karpeles nurtured a dream. Someday, he promised himself, he'd become a teacher. With a classroom filled with students eager to learn, he'd keep ahead of them by absorbing knowledge about many fields of endeavor. What a thrill it would be to impart understanding and skill to young people every day!

After graduation from Denfield High School in 1953, he enrolled at the University of Minnesota at Duluth where he received a bachelor's degree. Then he went to Saint Paul to work on a master's degree.

Well on the road toward reaching his boyhood dream, Karpeles married and found that his specialization in mathematics was opening doors he had not expected. Turning his back upon academia for the moment without completing the work for his advanced degree, he accepted a job offer from Remington Rand Univac, a firm noted for its pioneer work in the brand-new world of computers. This vocational change of direction was soon followed by a geographical shift when his employer sent him to California.

While working in the Golden State the man from the Land of Lakes transferred his credits, earned a master's degree, and began his studies for a Ph.D.

As he neared the finish line, he and his wife, Marsha, who was reared in the Twin Cities, woke up to the fact that his salary was big enough for them to invest in a piece of rental property. Still expecting one day to devote all of his time and energy to the classroom, Karpeles later said, "I couldn't help being aware of the huge number of boys and girls moving through school

David Karpeles is the son of a Duluth bus driver who has become an internationally known collector of manuscripts. [COURTESY OF DAVID KARPELES]

systems, but not yet widely known as baby boomers. Every one of them was a potential occupant of a rented or purchased home."

Realizing there would be a seller's market in housing by the time the baby boomers reached maturity, he bought another house, then another, and another, and another. "Soon I had so many houses on my hands that it took full time to look after them," he recalls from the distance of more than a quarter of a century.

One day late in the seventies, the two Minnesotans and their four teenage children visited an art museum in Pasadena. Most of the paintings and artifacts on display evoked a ho-hum reaction from the youngsters, but a display of old documents unexpectedly spurred their interest. Karpeles's son peered at an Albert Einstein manuscript and spontaneously blurted, "This is great! The father of the theory of relativity crossed out words and rewrote his sentences, just like I do!"

Real estate had brought the Duluth native so much money that he didn't know how best to invest it. This dilemma fused with the serendipitous reaction of his children to handwritten documents in a museum, and a passion was born. Karpeles

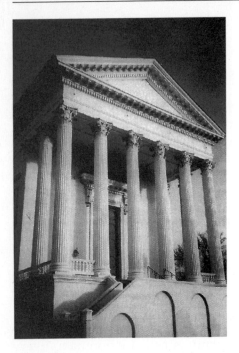

Charleston's Manuscript Library Museum at 68 Spring Street is housed in an elegant old building reminiscent of Robert E. Lee's Arlington and other mansions.

began surveying the market of manuscripts and historical documents with the combined interests of an investor-collector and a teacher outside the classroom. In 1978 he had pulled off an important purchase; the manuscript of Anthony H. Hawkins's novel *The Prisoner of Zenda* was his. Many a curator of a major museum would have relished this prize, but now it was the property of David Karpeles!

For a decade he pored over auction catalogs of rare documents. The son of a Duluth bus driver has become an internationally known collector of manuscripts, but he is reluctant to discuss his wealth and refuses to answer such questions as, "What did you pay for the piece you most prize? How much have you invested in your collection?"

Determined to acquire a 1787 letter written by Ethan Allen of American Revolutionary fame, he reputedly paid thirty-eight thousand dollars for the rare document. For much less he was able to purchase Thomas Edison's check paying an 1876 gas bill of $15.93. A letter from John Sutter, on whose property the California gold rush began, cost the Duluth native twenty-two

Closing lines of the Emancipation Proclamation, signed by Abraham Lincoln and penned by his secretary of state, William H. Seward.

thousand dollars. His first really big purchase, for which he is said to have spent forty thousand dollars, was the original draft of Abraham Lincoln's Emancipation Proclamation. Since he entered the market, interest in historic manuscripts and documents has multiplied, and values have jumped accordingly.

Today Karpeles holds one of the world's largest collections of original manuscripts—thousand upon thousand of them. Karpeles has made legal arrangements for his entire holdings to be accessible to the public without charge after his death. He owns the original draft of the lyrics of "The Star-Spangled Banner" as well as music that Beethoven wrote and a twelfth-century proclamation by Pope Lucius III prescribing a code of conduct for knights embarking on one of the crusades. His most valuable single piece, estimated by experts to be worth seven figures today, is the original U.S. Bill of Rights.

Harriet Beecher Stowe's novel about slavery had such an impact that a special Karpeles exhibit is at a Florida museum dedicated to her.

Karpeles owns and exhibits a first draft of the Constitution of the Confederate States of America, adopted in Montgomery, Alabama, in 1861. He also holds original-autograph copies of the national constitutions of Spain, France, Ireland, and Mexico. He is proud of a proclamation signed by George Washington naming November 26, 1789, a day of general thanksgiving, and believes that he has the only Final Declaration of Allegiance Treaty between the United States and its many Indian tribes. Martin Luther, who launched the Protestant Reformation, also is represented by one of his original documents.

By 1983 the University of Minnesota alumnus's long-delayed urge to teach became a reality in an unusual way. He opened a no-admission museum whereby he could effectively teach without going into a classroom. In Montecito, California, boys and girls flocked into the Karpeles Manuscript Library Museum to see and then to discuss twenty-five exhibits.

Karpeles then expanded his idea to other small cities. On a visit to his hometown for a high school class reunion, he spotted a For Sale sign in front of an abandoned church. Buying the once-elegant edifice for around two hundred thousand dollars, he then spent half as much on an elaborate renovation job, turning it into another Karpeles Museum. He now has manuscript libraries in Jacksonville, Tacoma/Seattle, Buffalo, Santa Barbara, and Charleston. Special exhibits have been placed in the Harriet Beecher Stowe Museum in Mandarin, Florida, and other specialized centers. Minimuseums are maintained in schools throughout the nation, where documents are changed every two months. Each permanent library, whose exhibits also rotate regularly, displays no more than twenty-five manuscripts at a time from such fields as history, music, science, literature, and art.

In each manuscript library, while the unseen presence of the investor-collector cannot be escaped, it is the would-be teacher who dominates. Because the Civil War began in Charleston, it seemed appropriate to send the Emancipation Proclamation to the opening of the learning facility there. Karpeles, the teacher, poses a number of questions in brochures that are handed out at each of his sites. Of South Carolina schoolchildren, he inquires whether an analysis of Abraham Lincoln's Emancipation Proclamation indicates that the document freed the slaves in America.

"Indeed it didn't," his answer to his own question correctly stipulates. Boys and girls who visit the Manuscript Library Museum learn that slavery was not officially abolished in the United States until the U.S. Constitution was amended.

Educational research indicates that information acquired informally outside the classroom is more lasting than the same data imparted by a teacher during a formal learning session. Karpeles, whose acquisition of a doctorate was interrupted by the boom in California housing, is certain that this is true. Hence he plans to continue expanding and displaying manuscripts as long as he has the money to do so.

24
Paul and Babe

Last of a Breed

"Where wuz you befo' you showed up on Rum River?"

That's mighty nigh the only question that ever got Paul Bunyan riled. Ever' time a green sawyer showed up in camp, sooner or later he'd ax that thar question. Just as sho as he did, Paul would go stompin' off through the woods, tryin' to work off his mad before he kilt sumbody.

Story goes that Paul and Babe, his blue ox, spent nigh onto a year way down in Virginie at a place named for a feller called Peter. Seems that General Ewe Esse Grant got into a passle of trouble with the Rebs, so somehow or t'other he got ahold of Paul and put him to work throwin' cannonballs. Babe hauled up freight cars loaded full of 460-pounders ever' mornin,' and soon as a few of them got red hot in the furnace ole Paul went to work. He rolled back his sleeves to keep 'em from gettin' scorched and chunked two or three to get the range. Then he spent the rest of the day makin' big trouble for the Rebs. At least, that's what some folks say 'bout the time before he showed up summers to the south of Mille Lacs Lake with Babe pullin' a sled 144 yards wide. That thar sled wuz loaded with a whole loggin' camp—640 tree fellers, ever' one of 'em luggin' a double-bladed ax an' chewin' coon skins 'cause they wuz fresh outta 'bacca.

That yarn, which emerged relatively late in the orally transmitted saga of Paul Bunyan and Babe the blue ox, is typical of many that preceded it. Exaggeration is a key motif of these stories. The hardy but vulnerable men who leveled the forests of Minnesota in the decades beginning about 1850 were a lot like the coal miner in "Tennessee" Ernie Ford's song. Day after day he dug sixteen tons and all the got was another day older and deeper in debt.

A few decades before Paul Bunyan became the central character of stories told around loggers' campfires, Davy Crockett's mighty accomplishments were the stock-in-trade of frontier yarn spinners. Soon afterward, river rats boasted a folk hero of their own named Mike Fink. John Henry, the steel-drivin' man, was to early railroaders what Crockett was to hunters and trappers and Fink was to men who spent their lives on the Ohio and Mississippi Rivers.

Paul Bunyan, who didn't surface until after the Civil War, was the last of a breed. No other folk hero of later vintage comes close to matching his size, his mighty muscles, or his incredible achievements that he recounted with yawns.

Coal miners, sharecroppers, frontiersmen, river rats, railroad builders, and lumbermen of the Northwest worked hard at difficult tasks from sunup to sundown for low wages without hope of advancement. For relief they sang work songs, chanteys, and the blues, and created wonder-workers to vicariously escape their dangerous and futile life cycles.

Many of the men whose axes toppled the forest giants of Minnesota were of Scandinavian origin. These woodsmen, say some psychologists, created Paul Bunyan as a "Thor of the Northwestern forests," a demigod dressed mostly in homespun and beaver hide with whom they could, in their imaginations, triumph over all obstacles.

No known story credits Paul with throwing a single thunderbolt as did Thor, the legendary Norse god. But his legend does report that often, at the end of a week when his men were coming up short, he swung his own immense ax for a couple of hours. Every single time he worked as a feller of trees, sweat poured from between his shoulders and down his back in such a stream that a brand-new creek was formed, cutting through several feet of earth as it rushed toward the nearest river.

One day about the middle of January, one story goes, a pair of greenhorns wandered into Paul's camp, which was empty because all of its members were working miles away. One of them came across a set of footprints. Shaking so violently he couldn't speak for an instant, he called for his companion to come running. Both of them stared in disbelief for a long moment before blurting simultaneously, "Bigfoot!" Then they

Paul Bunyan somehow managed
to keep a grin on his face nearly
all the time. [UNIVERSITY OF
MINNESOTA LIBRARIES]

hotfooted it back to Fort Snelling to tell their story to bug-eyed
listeners.

The master of the blue ox had a lot of muscular control, especially in his hands. His thumbs were as long as an ordinary
fellow's foot. And Babe was not his only animal companion. He
was crazy about Sport, a critter who was half elephant hound
and half wolf but who acted just like a good hunting dog.

One day when Sport was scratching his back against a pine
that measured more than four feet in diameter, Paul was working one of his special crosscut saws on the other side. Four ordinary saws, welded together, made a giant cutter so he could
rip through a two-footer in a quarter of an hour. Not noticing
that Sport was standing on his hind legs and leaning against

the far side of the tree, Paul gave a mighty surge with the saw, cutting plumb through the pine and then plumb through Sport.

As soon as he saw what he'd done, tenderhearted Paul Bunyan picked up both pieces of Sport in his arms and ran for camp, sobbing like a baby. He fumbled through his things, found a canvas needle already threaded, and before you could say Jack Robinson, old Sport was all sewed up, neat and tidy. The only trouble was, in his hurry the hind end of Sport got sewed onto his front end bottomside up.

When Babe was real thirsty, which was most of the time, that ox could drink a creek dry without taking a second breath. [UNIVERSITY OF MINNESOTA LIBRARIES]

Fifty-four sixteen-foot white pine logs were about as many as most loggers could get on a go-devil; with Babe hitched to his special skid, Paul once piled on 93,312.
[LIBRARY OF CONGRESS]

This was one of the few big mistakes Paul ever made, but it turned out well in the end. As soon as he got back on his feet, Sport found he could run on either his top or his bottom pair of legs, so from then on he never got tired. He could chase a deer for half a day and never start to pant. The truth of the matter was, from the time he was patched up after the accident, Sport caught every living thing he started after.

Another tale told how ordinary loggers would stack exactly fifty-four white pine logs, each sixteen feet long, on a sled that was pulled by a pair of horses. Lots of these loads were hauled all the way to the Mississippi River below the Falls of Saint Anthony. Then, after sitting for a while in a holding pond, they'd be loaded onto a special steamer and shipped downriver.

Paul wasn't much for steamers. He liked to hand peavies to river hogs and tell them to drive his logs to the nearest mill. Sometimes when they had a long way to go, the river was so full of two-legged hogs handling peavies that wanigans went along with them. Bull-cooks in these floating shacks worked around the clock feeding the crews so no time would be lost on the drive.

Logging historian Mary Jane Henniger worked for years trying to find out where Paul Bunyan and Babe came from and when they hit what tree fellers called "the edge of civilization." Writing in the *Journal of Forest History*, she concluded that newspaper reporter James H. MacGillivray published the first story about them in 1906. She found that it took three or four years for Paul to move from a weekly newspaper into the *Detroit News-Tribune*. After that, says Henniger, the mighty woodsman took off like a skyrocket. H. L. Mencken published Bunyan tales in the *American Mercury*. These tales inspired W. H. Auden, Carl Sandberg, and Robert Frost into writing long poems about his doings.

Nobody really knows for sure where Paul Bunyan came from or when. It's possible that French-Canadian fur trappers and traders of the Northwest told the earliest of all Paul Bunyan stories. They tried to resist when their territory was first invaded by woodsmen who cut the trees that sheltered the animals. Telling about Paul Bunyan and Babe helped them work off some of their frustration. This theory is buttressed by the fact that *Bon Jean*, meaning "brave John," was often slurred so it sounded a lot like *Boneyaahn*. *Boneyaahn* gradually became *Bonikon* and then *Bunyon* and eventually *Bunyan*, some scholars think.

To Minnesotans, it doesn't make much difference who told the first folk tales about the man and his ox. Regardless of where they originated, they were just right for the glory years when millions of board feet of timber went down the river from the Land of Lakes every season. Paul and his big crew of hired hands, along with Babe and Sport, spent a few seasons on the Big Onion River and a solid year in the Pyramid Forty Square Miles—locations somewhere in the heart of Minnesota forests that city dwellers can't find today.

That being the case, it's logical that the Bemidji-Brainerd snow country, just north of Minnesota 18, should have a statue of Paul Bunyan that towers practically as tall as a lighthouse and, like the folk hero, never shirks its duty of welcoming visitors to the region.

Part 5

Far Beyond State Borders

Lynne Rosetto Kasper of "The Splendid Table." [MPR]

25
MPR

www.mpr.org

Kari Rise, Dean Westberg, and Grant Ault were having a great time as pages in the sergeant's office at the Minnesota House of Representatives. Even though they were weary from another week of strenuous duties, they found enough time and energy to send an e-mail message about their experience to Minnesota Public Radio (MPR).

A mutual friend who is a small-time pig farmer living near Austin is also a dyed-in-the-wool radio buff who keeps his radio going nonstop, they reported. One afternoon when he was listening to rock and roll and country music, he noticed that his animals "became restless and agitated." Turning to the clear, classical sounds on MPR, their owner watched with astonishment as his pigs relaxed so quickly that they soon went to sleep for the night. These four-legged dedicated listeners, suggested Kari, "deserve special recognition."

That yarn, which *may* have been influenced by frequent periods of loafing at the Side Tap in Lake Wobegon (see chapter 10, "Garrison Keillor: Lake Wobegon") was in one of hundreds of letters sent by listeners who were delighted when MPR was launched in 1967. That was the year Congress passed a public broadcasting act aimed at broadening the scope of noncommercial use of the airways. At that time the future of public radio was far from clear. The proliferation of television, it was predicted, would "soon make radio obsolete."

It would seem now that just the opposite has happened. MPR's senior economic and business editor, Chris Farrell, noted in 1996 that while public radio faces "intense competition for private dollars," in the radio field as a whole, "advertising revenues soared almost 30 percent." Investment bankers Varanus, Sutler & Associates have predicted that until the turn of the century radio will grow faster than any other measured medium.

Some regular listeners to one of the MPR stations serving the state and adjacent regions tend to take their radio fare for granted. Many do not know that the flawless music of *Saint Paul Sunday* also is enjoyed in the South Carolina Low Country and that MPR's *Sound Money* advises freeway-driving investors in LA as well as throughout Minnesota.

Anywhere that the Internet is available, computer users log on to MPR's Website—www.mpr.org—to hear, and even enjoy the offerings from an enormous audio selection of tantalizing tidbits, popular staples, and innovative surprises. Only one adjective—*stupendous!*—is suitable to characterize www.mpr.org.

It's no surprise that MPR's Website has links to Websites for five nationally distributed programs: *A Prairie Home Companion*, *Sound Money*, *Future Tense*, *Saint Paul Sunday*, and *The Splendid Table of Lynne Rosetto Kasper*. All of these programs inspire interaction with listeners in Minnesota and around the world, so each has its own e-mail address to receive listener feedback. The Website's archives—which change frequently—are likely to include a score of news features and several musical features

One memorable archive developed early in the spring of 1997, when MPR staffers with long memories sensed that something big was about to happen. Few expected, however, that the news staff would soon be covering "the flood of the century." The rampage of the Red River of the North and the flood's aftermath continued for ten weeks unlike any comparable period on record. MPR was there from beginning to end.

Minnesotans who lived far away as well as those who were fascinated by the disaster and its ensuing relief efforts stayed informed with sixty separate news features, each with transcript plus RealAudio, in the Website's archives for use throughout the nation.

As big as it was, the flood of the century wasn't the only topic offered on MPR's Website; two dozen other news and musical features were there to inform and entertain visitors as well. A three-part series on the life of composer Clara Schumann was offered for MPR's music lovers, in competition with a celebration of the two hundredth anniversary of Franz Schubert's birth

*Minnesota Public Radio
President William H. Kling.*
[MPR]

and a selection of limericks that linked Beethoven with Emerson. Frances Densmore's collection of Native American music offered audio, movies, and even a magic lantern show.

Other intriguing MPR offerings have included a piece by Stephen Smith, a senior reporter-producer of national projects, who came up with a fast-moving account of "Shaped Note Singing—a southern tradition that thrives in the North." This communal form of music flourished long ago in New England, Smith explained, then gradually drifted southward and took root in rural communities. Very early in the nineteenth century, at least two publishers issued songbooks with distinctively shaped notes, making it possible for a devotee to tell the pitch of a note by a glance.

MPR's Website and e-mail addresses are among the ways the broadcasters stay attuned with their listeners. Susan S. Boren, who recently rotated out of office as chair of the MPR board of trustees, calls listeners "a large, mostly unseen group that the board talks about at each meeting." Because only a fraction of the national base of listeners give financial support directly to

MPR, board president William H. Kling couldn't conceal his delight at telling board members that for fifteen consecutive fiscal years MPR had ended "in the black."

In a move that some regarded as bold and others considered rash, MPR recently set out to convert its studios for computerized digital broadcast production. That couldn't possibly have been achieved without a major capital funds campaign—which brought in $11 million. Most of the big gifts—$100,000 and above—came from foundations and corporations, but hundreds of smaller gifts were essential to reaching the goal as well.

A summary of the capital campaign—which was completely independent of regular campaigns for operating funds—stressed a central matter that helps explain MPR's success:

> There are few communities where the value of public radio has been understood as well as it is here—and even fewer where public radio is considered a significant community institution that merits major philanthropic support.

U.S. Census Bureau figures, updated to April 1994, indicate that 4.3 million Minnesotans are spread out over 79,617 square miles in which twenty-four stations and eighteen local translators provide MPR programs. An additional five stations are located outside the state. Minnesota has more National Public Radio–member stations—fifteen—than any other state in the entire nation. California, twice as large and with nearly seven times as many residents, has only eleven such stations. About seventeen million Texans, spread out over 261,000 square miles, have just five NPR stations to listen to. When combined, the nine stations in Illinois and six in New York are precisely equal in number to Minnesota's fifteen.

MPR is in every sense a true national treasure whose programs and Website are available from coast to coast and border to border.

26
Havoc in the Heartland
Creative Conflict

Frank Ellis tried to play a low-key role when, along with dozens of other members of his Independent Union of All Workers (IUAW), he stormed into the Hormel packing plant in Austin, Minnesota, at 10:00 P.M. on November 10, 1933. When the company's president saw club-wielding strikers headed toward his office, he decided that physical resistance would be futile, so he quickly "went limp." Shouting words of assurance to one another, several workers picked up their boss and jubilantly carried him out of the plant.

Ellis, formerly a general organizer for the radical Industrial Workers of the World (IWW, or Wobblies), began "talking union" soon after he joined the company's casing department. Since he considered no existing body of organized labor to be quite right for the Austin situation, he quietly planned his IUAW and put it into motion without seeking a charter for it. In what would otherwise have been a routine meeting of the union on the evening of payday, two red-hot issues reached the boiling point.

Management had initially followed the customary pattern of paying workers monthly, but for a number of years they had been paid on an hourly system. In 1931, the fortieth year of the business, the company decided to experiment with what was then called "straight time" payment, now termed an annual wage. Experimentally, workers in two departments were considered to be permanently on the payroll, short of serious infractions, and were assured that the averaging of peak and slack periods would mean a forty-hour work week during a year. Since the new method of keeping time and paying wages seemed to mean progress for all concerned, it was gradually expanded in spite of the fact that some employees complained about it.

A second managerial innovation was widely resented. "Why on the top side of earth do owners think they can get away with stashing away some of a man's pay for his old age?" Ellis demanded stridently.

In the depth of the Great Depression, it seemed foolish to talk about the mandatory launching of a company pension plan. The payroll deduction for this purpose served as the match to light a bonfire in otherwise tranquil Austin. Workers went on strike, demanding abolition of the pension plan and a pay raise of ten cents an hour.

After having cleared the company's general offices on November 10, members of the IUAW decided that more radical action was needed. Someone yelled, "Let's shut down the refrigeration!" The proposal was received with enthusiasm, and it was quickly implemented by men accustomed to operating the system. Now in full possession of the entire plant, the strikers occupied every department in shifts.

There was no violence of the sort that had marked earlier strikes in the East, and physical damage to the plant was small. Because workers were present but not performing their customary duties, their takeover entered the record books as the first modern sit-down strike. With Austin as the center, the IUAW succeeded in establishing branches in a number of nearby cities.

Less than four years later, clerks at a Woolworth store in Albert Lea decided to employ the device that had made national news from the packing plant about eighteen miles to their east. Their sit-down strike triggered two more at American Gas Machine Company plants in Albert Lea. Before the year ended, members of the United Auto Workers followed the Minnesota precedent and won recognition of their union from one of the world's largest industrial enterprises, General Motors.

Ellis and the IUAW members who followed his leadership didn't realize in November 1933 that they were making labor history by remaining at their places while refusing to work. They did know that they were in excellent bargaining position, because meat worth $3.6 million would soon reach a temperature at which it would spoil.

Since the strike threatened the economy of the state, civil

authorities eyed it with a combination of fear and anger. All deputies of the Mower County Sheriff's Department were called into duty, and three hundred members of the National Guard were ordered to Austin. A reporter for the *Daily Herald* gave his assessment of the climate of public opinion: "With the plant in control of the strikers, the refrigeration system turned off, and a call made for National Guard and federal troops, the people's anxiety reached a pitch Saturday night that was probably never equaled in the history of the city."

Gov. Floyd B. Olson reached the site of the growing crisis less than forty-eight hours after the sit-down began and put his weight behind a negotiated settlement.

As a result, both the company and the IUAW agreed to defer to the Minnesota State Industrial Commission, with refrigeration being turned on and work being resumed without waiting for verdicts from that body. Formal settlement of the management-labor dispute gave concessions to both sides. Rejecting the demand for a 25 percent increase in hourly wages, the commission awarded workers a five-cent, instead of a ten-cent, raise—from forty to forty-five cents an hour. The annual wage plan was discontinued by the company, which also agreed that no striker would lose his or her job. In turn, members of the IUAW resumed their normal duties on Monday morning.

The first modern sit-down strike probably would have erupted into violence had it occurred a few years earlier. Violent clashes between management and labor had left huge scars upon cities and states in which they took place. In 1877 a strike by Pennsylvania's anthracite coal miners ended after six bitter months because hunger forced the workers to accept a 20 percent cut in wages. When a number of major railroads announced wage cuts during the same period, a revolt that started in Baltimore spread elsewhere. In Philadelphia, members of the state militia opened fire on a crowd of twenty thousand demonstrators, and President Rutherford B. Hayes reacted by calling out federal troops—a step he took repeatedly. Railroad service was restored nationwide on August 2, after scores of strikers and their sympathizers had been killed and uncounted hundreds had been injured.

In the second half of the nineteenth century, formation of the Knights of Labor marked the real beginning of the modern movement to organize workers for better working conditions.

By 1886 the Knights had about seven hundred thousand members, mostly concentrated in Chicago. Numerous strikes were launched on May Day in 1886, and nearly half of them achieved some of their stated goals.

Among those that failed was a Knights of Labor attempt to get an eight-hour workday at the McCormick International Harvester Company. During two or three days, Chicago police killed at least four strikers, and on May 6 a rally in support of the strikers was staged at Haymarket Square just south of the city's center. The massed throng of demonstrators was charged by a platoon of police who ordered the crowd to disperse. A dynamite bomb, allegedly thrown by an anarchist, killed seven persons and injured sixty-seven others. Four more were killed when police fired a volley.

Eight persons accused of complicity in the bombing went on trial. Four of them were executed, one committed suicide in prison, and the remaining three received life sentences. National horror over the Haymarket Square incident and its aftermath caused the Knights of Labor and the movement for an eight-hour workday to go into a decline.

Andrew Carnegie's vast steel mill at Homestead, Pennsylvania, was closed when workers refused to accept an 1892 cut in wages. Pinkerton detectives filled two barges that were fired upon as they approached Homestead. After a pitched battle, the strikebreakers were forced to retreat, at which point the governor of Pennsylvania sent eight thousand militiamen to the site of the struggle. Once the armed guardsmen were in control, the company brought in nonunion "scabs" to replace the four thousand strikers, of whom only eight hundred were eventually rehired.

Two years later workers building sleeping cars for the George M. Pullman Company struck when a 22 percent wage cut was announced. Soon the local workers' strike was joined by 150,000 members of the American Railway Union. Federal troops sent to Chicago by President Grover Cleveland and state militia units filled the city with fourteen thousand soldiers, and the strike was broken. In its aftermath Eugene V. Debs of the Railway Union went to jail for violation of a court order. Angrily turning to the tiny Socialist Party, he won its nomination for the presidency and received nearly one million votes from his cell in Atlanta's federal prison.

Pennsylvania coal miners who supported labor unions were widely known as Molly Maguires, and in 1874 had to meet in secret. [HARPER'S WEEKLY]

Dramatic defeats suffered by organized labor sent the movement into decline despite the fact that Labor Day became a legal holiday in 1894. At the turn of the century, only about 3 percent of the nation's seventeen million industrial workers belonged to unions. In a climate of heated opposition to organized labor, a survey found that four out of every ten textile workers in New England were children ranging in age from four to fourteen. "Little children" were earning one dollar a week, while older women, known as "Lowell girls," were paid two or three dollars. Textile workers in Lawrence, Massachusetts, went on strike in 1912 and quickly found themselves facing members of the state militia. This fracas ended when a clash between police and strikers led to the death of an adult woman.

Before the decade was over, a major law enforcement body went on strike in the same state. In 1919 the city of Boston refused to recognize the policemen's union and would not enter into negotiations about a new wage scale. Soon after members of the police force walked off the job, Gov. Calvin Coolidge broke the strike by using the state guard, and the

On May 4, 1886, a bomb exploded in the midst of persons who were staging a rally in support of strikers. [HAYMARKET]

union of officers went out of existence. Many officials holding state and national posts condemned the union movement everywhere it existed.

As much as any other American, Franklin D. Roosevelt was responsible for a change in public opinion. In 1933 his National Industrial Recovery Act stressed the right of workers to engage in collective bargaining, and soon a National Labor Board was established to serve as mediator in disputes. Membership in the United Mine Workers, the Amalgamated Clothing Workers, and other national organizations soared. Meanwhile, dozens of small and independent unions like the IUAW were formed, and most of them functioned without violence.

Then a 1937 Chicago strike led by members of the young but powerful Committee for Industrial Organization (CIO) within the American Federation of Labor brought another violent clash between workers and police. Squads of uniformed officers, wielding both billy clubs and guns, waded into picket lines on Memorial Day and left ten demonstrators dead and many others injured.

By 1975 the George A. Hormel Company had experienced rapid growth, leading to the establishment of a network of plants. The Austin facility remained central to the operation although it was approaching obsolescence. The company was paying the highest wages in the industry under a new guaranteed annual wage system. Workers also received incentive pay through a joint earnings program that gave them a portion of company profits. This management-worker arrangement in Austin was considered ideal, and it had been called "the best large-company work climate in the Western world."

With a new Austin plant seen as essential to continued operation in the city of the Hormel Company's origins, management concluded that the cost of the new plant ruled out additional wage increases for workers. By this time the once-independent IUAW had been replaced by Local 9 of the United Packinghouse Workers of America. Operating under the umbrella of the AFL–CIO, this national organization merged with others and became the United Food and Commercial Workers Union (UFCW). Local 9, however, soon began feuding with the new UFCW.

Negotiations for a new contract, launched in 1975, seemed to be near the point of collapse after three years. Then union leaders, faced with the fact that the Austin facility might be closed, accepted a plan for transition into a new plant and promised not to strike for three years after it went into operation. This agreement seems to have rested upon mutual understanding that Hormel workers would receive "industry wage rates," calculated from compiling reports by all major packing houses.

On June 25, 1979, construction started on the huge new facility. Soon after full production began, Hormel's competitors began cutting prices. To meet the competition, in the summer of 1984, workers in all Hormel plants were told their wages would be reduced by 23 percent—to an average of $8.25 an hour. This produced angry reactions by all union members. Eventually the anger boiled over into a strike in August 1985, following the release of a rewritten management-worker agreement on July 17.

Standing at far right with his arms folded, in 1898, George A. Hormel is not visibly different from fellow workers who are his employees. [Hormel Foods Corporation]

After a bitter contest that lasted five months and brought no results, management announced the reopening of the Austin plant on January 13, 1986. Strikers were urged to return to work and warned that unless they did so they could lose their jobs to "permanent replacements."

Members of numerous other labor organizations became involved and on January 20 helped to shut down the plant by a motor blockade from Minneapolis and Saint Paul. In a bizarre modification of the 1933 strike, the offices of the governor were invaded, and prolabor demonstrators launched a sit-in that lasted for several weeks. Soon members of the state highway patrol and the National Guard arrived in Austin, ready to escort strikebreakers to their new jobs when the plant reopened.

By February, an estimated 450 union members who had decided to cross picket lines and numerous new employees were ready to go to work. Out-of-state supporters of the strike, which was still a subject of hot dispute between the local unions involved, flocked to Minnesota and began staging demonstrations. With tension continuing to mount, county and city law enforcement officers resorted to use of tear gas on April 11, and they arrested seventeen people on felony riot charges. The resolution of a lawsuit filed by the UFCW signaled the demise of Local 9 as an independent entity. Sporadic nonviolent clashes continued until the summer of 1987, by that time the Austin plant had only workers who chose to return to their jobs rather than retire or seek other employment.

Throughout the nation, analysts of labor struggles bemoaned the long period of "havoc in the heartland" and pointed out that prior to its outbreak, Hormel's operations in Austin were considered to be "a model for the industry." Precisely how and why so long and bitter a struggle should have taken place in what was once a cohesive small city dominated by a single industry remains a matter of inquiry and discussion.

Film maker Barbara Kopple's treatment, entitled *American Dream*, includes many gross errors of fact and is conspicuous for what it omits. *American Dream*, along with numerous treatments of the strike in print media, fails to deal with the economic struggle faced by long-prominent corporations in the packing industry.

The bitter strike in Austin was a sign of the economic struggles several other commercial meatpacking companies were facing during those turbulent economic years. Barely twenty miles from Austin, Wilson and Company closed its Albert Lea plant in 1983 and 1,350 workers became jobless. Such famous names as Rath, Armour, Swift, and Cudahy no longer appear in financial publications because they have gone under or have become components of conglomerates. At one time, three corporations of the packing industry were listed in the top ten of the Fortune 500 list; now none are represented there. Intense economic pressure upon management was a major but often overlooked factor of "the strike no one expected."

Some aspects of the tangled and complex management-labor situation at Hormel's Austin operation are still subjects of debate, but one conclusion is inescapable. So long as tension between management and labor does not erupt violently, the end results of conflict are likely to be creative enough to benefit all parties. When the level of tension rises to the point where it cannot be contained, as it did half a century after that historic sit-down strike in Austin, a high price will be paid by most persons involved.

27
Greyhound Bus Origin
The Snoose Line

At the Pentagon, specialists who concentrate upon raw materials essential for modern military efforts say that without Minnesota, the United States might have been defeated in World War II. From the immense iron reserves concentrated in and north of Saint Louis County, Minnesota, which forms the Mesabi Iron Range, came an estimated 40 to 50 percent of the high-grade iron needed to defeat Germany and Japan. At the peak of its production during the 1940s, about one-fourth of all the iron produced in the nation came from a single mine in this range—the enormous Hull-Rust Mahoning Mine, one of the largest open-pit, iron mines in the world.

Frank Hibbing, about whom few details are positively known, had a hunch that something worth money was under the ground in the region now traversed by U.S. 169 and Minnesota 73. He discounted rumors that Indians once gathered gold in the general area and on December 29, 1891, took out a lease to mine iron ore.

The first such lease in the region persuaded a handful of pioneers to name their tiny settlement for him. In 1895 the operators of an open pit, or strip, mine shipped their first trainload of ore to the East, where all of the nation's big mills were located. On the first leg of its journey, the ore traveled along the Duluth River, the Mississippi River, and the Northern Logging Railroad. At Superior, Wisconsin, it was transferred to heavy-duty vessels that took it to a railhead linked with a mill. World War I created a huge demand for iron. Industrialist Elbert H. Gary, who organized the United States Steel Corporation in 1901 with Andrew Carnegie, visited Washington and made a personal pledge to President Woodrow Wilson. The tycoon said, "Sir, I know how badly you need iron. Have no fear; you will get all you can use—and more!"

Gary's promise meant a great deal. His and Carnegie's U.S. Steel Corporation's Oliver Iron Mining division acquired the already noted Hull-Rust Mine and supplied money and equipment to double and then redouble its output. The expansion of the surface mine, or pit, was so rapid that its edge was soon at the town of Hibbing. Correctly believing that great quantities of valuable ore lay beneath the village, the executives pushed for immediate expansion of the mine.

Demand for iron ore of high quality was so great that a half-century endeavor got under way in 1906. That's when a few wooden buildings at the edge of Hibbing were mounted on steel wheels and moved about two miles to the south. There they formed the nucleus of a new community known as Alice. During the dozen years following 1912, numerous other structures were moved, and brick buildings like the courthouse and schools were torn down. Structures that lay outside the mining zone remained in place, now separated both from familiar shops and businesses and from homes that "went south" in the move.

In 1914 two area residents pooled their assets and bought a seven-passenger open-air touring Hupmobile. Charlie Wenberg, a salesman for Aetna Powder Company, didn't have time to devote to their car, so his partner, Andrew G. Anderson, used their vehicle as a demonstration model to sell cars to the public.

Anderson had numerous requests for trial rides from prospective customers, but none of them bought a car. With the value of the vehicle dropping rapidly because of its frequent use on the rough roads of the day, the two investors became discouraged. Then Charlie's father, John Wenberg, suggested, "Instead of giving free rides, why not charge for them?"

This was a great moment in the history of transportation. On the following day the Hupmobile was parked at its customary location, but a sign on it proclaimed: "Hibbing to Alice—15 cents one way and 25 cents round trip."

Numerous residents jumped at the chance of a quick and comfortable ride between Hibbing and the town it had spawned. As a result, the car that nobody wanted to buy brought its owners

The Pierce Great Arrow Touring car was an early rival of the Hupmobile, now seen only at Hibbing and a handful of other museums. [HANDBOOK OF GASOLINE AUTOMOBILES (1908)]

$11.50 on the first day it went into service as a passenger carrier. On the following day, the owners of the converted Hup cleared $7.40 after having paid for gas. The next day their net take jumped to $20. The success of the Hibbing-to-Alice run prompted the partners to add other routes to their line.

It wasn't long before so many would-be passengers began showing up that the big automobile couldn't accommodate all of them. Carl Heed, a friend of the entrepreneurs, owned a Buick, and he and his car were invited to join the thriving transportation business.

Success almost always breeds competition, and that was the case in Hibbing. Ralph Bogan, the owner of a Studebaker, soon began a passenger line between Hibbing and Chisholm. When he cut his rates, his competitors followed suit. That meant all of them began to lose money, so Bogan joined the others in what became the Hibbing Transportation Company. As business expanded, more cars and drivers were added, and Andrew Anderson acquired the nickname "bus," short for omnibus.

No one recorded the name of the jokester who first complained, "Hibbing Transportation Company is too high and mighty." The rider suggested to his fellow passengers, "Let's

The 1914 Hupmobile ready for its first run and not yet crammed full of paying passengers. [Greyhound Bus Origin Center]

come down to earth and call this outfit the 'Snoose Line.'" His fellow passengers roared with laughter, lifted their hands in mock toasts to the "Snoose Line."

Since few outsiders were patrons, those who relied upon the "Snoose Line" needed no explanation. Snoose is the Swedish word for snuff, a tobacco product then popular with men. Many patrons of what was beginning to be known as a bus line were heavy users. When one of them perched on his seat with puffed-up lips leaned over to spit, his fellow passengers had to dodge.

An old photograph shows the original Hup crowded with passengers, including men sitting on the fenders and standing on the running boards. Even when the owners decided to stretch their vehicle, the additional space wasn't enough. When word reached Hibbing that a company had discovered how to place a bus body on the chassis of a White truck, two of these vehicles were purchased. Scheduled to make its first run, the bus prototype refused to budge. The weight of the passengers caused the body to settle upon its tires, and it wouldn't move. Taken to the company's new body shop, an additional leaf was inserted in the springs, and the bus began operating with full loads of passengers.

The general public, some of whom never boarded the Hup or

The Hupmobile (right) is dwarfed by succeeding generations of buses, each of which became larger and more elegant. [GREYHOUND BUS ORIGIN CENTER]

the other vehicles that soon joined the bus line, took pride in its operation. During the first harsh Minnesota winters in which the "Snoose Line" was in operation, the White trucks sometimes got stuck in snow. When farmers saw this situation, they would hitch up a team of horses and pull the vehicles to hard ground. In true entrepreneurial fashion, the owners turned to Bogan's father, an experienced boilermaker. He designed a blade that could be fitted to the front of the improvised bus, and with it the partners often cleared snow-covered roads. "They plowed the roads long before the state or county started this practice," according to an old-timer, "and also put up snow fences."

By December 15, 1915, the transportation company had grown so much that it was incorporated as the Mesabi Transportation Company. Swan Sinistrum, Mike Kramer, Ed Extreme, and other men joined the company, and by 1916 eighteen buses were in operation. These owners continued to expand their tiny fleet.

Walkman and Heed sold out in Hibbing and helped to organize the Superior White Bus Company in Superior, Wisconsin, because they knew that many rural communities were in need of reliable transportation. When others who had taken part in the Hibbing experiment joined them, they formed the Motor Transit Corporation and decided to go after big money. Executives of the Great Northern Railroad were interested in the Hibbing experiment and the wide-open transportation market. In February 1925 they responded by helping to plan a greatly expanded network of routes and investing $2.5 million in buses. Soon 150 buses were rolling over twenty-five hundred miles of rural routes. Thus the Greyhound bus system was born.

Walkman rejoiced that tens of thousands of persons in hundreds of isolated communities could now travel to the outside world and back by means of the Motor Transit Corporation, but he chafed at "nuisance delays" suffered by passengers. Most of these were due to the fact that when a person went any distance, he was likely to change bus companies several times—requiring him to buy new tickets and transfer luggage at each change. "What we need," he told fellow executives in an expansive mood, "is a network in which a person can go coast-to-coast and border-to-border on a single ticket."

When that goal was announced, it seemed all but impossible to achieve. However, the Greyhound Transportation Corporation, today based in Dallas, and its eleven thousand employees have converted the dream of nationwide travel on a single ticket into a reality so familiar that it seems almost humdrum.

At the birthplace of the Greyhound bus system, a museum was established in 1989 to preserve and tell its story. Today there are five restored historical buses on exhibition: the 1914 Hupmobile, a 1936 Supercoach, a 1948 Silverside, and a 1956 Scenicruiser. Pictorial and audiovisual displays, along with artifacts and memorabilia, help visitors to understand the beginning of passenger-bus evolution.

Plans are under way to erect a new building that will be situated on Greyhound Boulevard in Hibbing. In 1984 this stretch of road was formally named and dedicated, since it is part of the route taken by the 1914 Hup on its first trip from Hibbing to Alice with passengers aboard. Until the new building is completed, visitors will find the Greyhound Bus Origin Center at Twenty-third Street and Fifth Avenue in Hibbing. For information call 218-263-5814. The museum is open five days a week from mid-May through September.

No known vehicle comes anywhere close to matching the record set by the Hupmobile that is on display at the center. A single vehicle that no one wanted to buy has spawned thousands of buses that have grown bigger and more comfortable with each passing generation.

Three Hundred Years of First Events and Achievements

Circa 1603—Following the instructions of King Henry IV of France, Samuel de Champlain ascends the Saint Lawrence River as far as possible then travels by land, possibly becoming the first European to set foot in what is now Minnesota.

Circa 1659–1661—Pierre Esprit Radisson and Médard Chouart, Sieur des Groseilliers, reach the Upper Mississippi on a fur-trading expedition.

1669—Robert Cavelier, better known as the Sieur de La Salle, passes through part of Minnesota during an expedition to the region of Lake Ontario.

1679—French native Daniel Greysolon, Sieur Duluth (or Du Lhut), persuades Indian chieftains to attend a peace council then claims the region for King Louis XIV.

1680—Father Johannes (Louis) Hennepin, a native of Flanders, explores the region around Mille Lacs and becomes the first European to see the Falls of Saint Anthony.

1670—The region around Grand Portage is firmly established as the center of the vast North American fur trade.

1782—Starting from Canada, La Salle reaches the Gulf of Mexico on April 9 and claims the Mississippi River Valley for France, naming this vast region Louisiana in honor of Louis XIV.

1783—American and British commissioners sign the Treaty of Paris, ending the American Revolution. One of the issues is that of geographical boundaries, complicated by French and Spanish claims.

Consulting a faulty map issued in 1755, the negotiators agree that a boundary between the United States and what is left of British North America should start at the western head of Lake Superior. From that point, the boundary follows a number of rivers to "the most Northwestern point of the Lake of the Woods." Then the line moves due west to the Mississippi River, which the map shows as rising north of the Lake of the Woods.

Later surveys reveal that the Father of Waters originates at Lake Itasca, about 150 miles south of the Lake of the Woods. An international dispute over the faulty boundary line erupts in 1792, and two years later a new treaty provides that a joint commission shall study and resolve the issue; however, the commission never meets.

After the War of 1812, a new commission decrees that the boundary line shall proceed from the northern tip of the Lake of the Woods to latitude 49 degrees North and follow that path to the Rocky Mountains. In 1846 still another treaty extends the northern edge of the United States along that latitude to the Pacific Ocean.

Thus the boundary between the United States and Canada dips southward from the Lake of the Woods and then proceeds due west. Today a few Minnesotans live near Angle Point, just above Red Lake Reservation, at the northernmost spot in the contiguous states.

1783—Although Britain has yielded her claim to the land, British entrepreneurs make their North West Company the dominant force among competing fur traders of the region.

1787—A congressional ordinance places much of eastern Minnesota in the Northwest Territory.

1804—Thomas Jefferson dispatches Meriwether Lewis and William Clark to explore the land acquired through the Louisiana Purchase.

September 1805—Lt. Zebulon M. Pike reaches the Minnesota country during his exploration of the Upper Mississippi Valley. He raises the first United States flag to fly on Minnesota soil and persuades the Sioux to cede land for the erection of army posts.

1819—At the junction of the Minnesota and Mississippi Rivers, Fort Saint Anthony is built as the northernmost post of the U.S. Army. Soon renamed Fort Snelling, for decades it is the chief outpost of the United States in the Upper Mississippi River region.

*Lieutenant Zebulon M. Pike
discovered Pike's Peak a few
years after leaving Minnesota.*
[ENGRAVING AFTER CHARLES
WILLSON PEALE PORTRAIT]

1820—Soldiers stationed at Fort Snelling decide to experiment with a crop they hope will be suitable for the climate of Minnesota. They plant and harvest wheat.

1820—Wives of some of the military officers stationed at Fort Snelling decide that their children need formal instruction, so they establish and teach in the state's first school.

1821—The first farmers who settle in the rich agricultural region around Fort Snelling are Swiss immigrants.

1823—Minnesota's first mill for the production of flour and grist is built, powered by water flowing through the Falls of Saint Anthony.

1823—Steamboat travel on the Minnesota section of the Mississippi River is launched.

1823—U.S. Army engineer Stephen H. Long makes a leisurely journey down the Red River of the North after having reached it by traveling up the Mississippi.

1830s—Artist George Catlin visits the pipestone quarry.

1830s—Missionaries Jedediah D. Stevens, Samuel Pond, and Gideon Pond start a school at Lake Harriet for Native American children.

1830s—Lumbering on a small commercial scale begins in forests along the Saint Croix River.

1839—At Grand Portage, Catholics establish the state's first school for the children of Chippewas.

1849—Saint Paul incorporates as a town, becoming the capital of the new Minnesota Territory, with Alexander Ramsey the first governor of the territory. James M. Goethic launches the *Minnesota Pioneer* as the region's first newspaper. Around four thousand white persons are living in Minnesota when it becomes a territory.

1851–55—An 1851 treaty with the Sioux, followed by 1854 and 1855 treaties with the Chippewa, makes immense tracts of land available to settlers in the Minnesota Territory. As a result, the population increases by 2,500 percent in a seven-year period.

May 11, 1858—Minnesota becomes the thirty-second state of the Union, with a population around 150,000. Henry H. Sibley, a Democrat, is the first governor of the state (1858–1860).

April 29, 1861—Minnesota provides the first regiment of volunteer soldiers, the First Minnesota, to fight for the Union. On the day after the firing on Fort Sumter, Gov. Alexander Ramsey offers the unit to the secretary of war, Simon Cameron.

December 26, 1861—At Mankato, Sioux Indians are the central figures in the first (and last) U.S. mass execution in which more than three dozen convicted men die simultaneously.

1862—The Saint Paul and Pacific Railroad begins operation with the state's first steam-propelled locomotives.

1864—Count Ferdinand von Zeppelin, a German observer of the U.S. Civil War, reaches Fort Snelling. He would later conduct experiments in lighter-than-air craft, large versions of which would someday bear his name.

December 4, 1867—In Washington, D.C., Oliver H. Kelley plays a central role in the organization of the Order of the Patrons of Husbandry, generally known as the Grange. It is the first general farm organization in the United States.

1869—Led by the bishop of Minnesota, Henry B. Whipple, residents of Faribault and adjoining regions, and Episcopalians throughout the United States complete construction of the first Episcopal cathedral in the nation. It costs more than $100,000, the equivalent of about $4 million today.

1870—The great Minnesota lumber boom, destined to last for three decades, begins as a result of newly built railroads.

The Falls of St. Anthony as they appeared in 1856.

January 1876—Saint Paul resident E. F. Drake is instrumental in organizing the nation's first state forestry association. Its chief aim is to promote reforestation. For this end the legislature appropriates twenty-five thousand dollars.

1880—The census shows that Minnesota is heavily rural and is first among the states in its ethnic mix of citizens with European roots, with 71 percent of Minnesotans being first- or second-generation Europeans. At least twelve nations are heavily represented: Germany, Sweden, Norway, Poland, Finland, France, Holland, Iceland, Denmark, Switzerland, Great Britain, and Ireland.

January 18, 1884—William H. Fruen of Minneapolis applies for a patent to be used by drugstore soda clerks to reduce guesswork by automatically dispensing a preset amount of a liquid intended for refreshment.

1884—Men coming to Minnesota in search of gold find no deposits of value, but iron ore is visible to the naked eye in the Vermilion Range. The hunt for metal intensifies, and soon the Mesabi and Cuyanga Ranges are found and large-scale mining of iron ore gets under way.

The Cathedral of Our Merciful Saviour, the first Episcipal cathedral in the United States, Faribault, Minnesota [COURTESY OF THE CATHEDRAL OF OUR MERCIFUL SAVIOUR]

1884—New Ulm Catholics erect the first hillside shrine in the United States, "the Way of the Cross." The Minnesota landmark inspires numerous other groups to create chapels that can be seen from the roadside.

Circa 1885—Throughout the United States, Minneapolis is recognized as the premier flour-milling city of the nation.

1886—Near Red Wing around two dozen skiers organize the nation's first ski club, choosing Christ Boxrud as their president. By the time the February snow is heavy in 1887, they are ready to stage an invitational meet featuring two Norwegians with international reputations.

October 1888—The University of Minnesota starts a vocational agricultural school. The first of its kind in the United States, it is soon copied by other land-grant universities.

June 1891—A new ship design, appropriately known as "the whale-back steamer," makes its maiden voyage from Duluth. More than 250 feet long, the steamer *Charles W. Whitmore* transports more than one thousand tons of grain to Liverpool in near-record time.

1892—Theophilus L. Haecker leads in the organization of cooperative creameries, the first of which becomes fully operative in 1889. With the transition from wheat farming to dairy farming, Minnesota is becoming the chief butter-producing state in the nation.

June 6, 1892—Minnesotans, already nationally noted for their encouragement of female participation in political processes, give a special welcome to a pair of Wyoming women who reach Minneapolis on this day. Both are delegates to the tenth national convention of the Republican Party, scheduled to begin tomorrow. When they set foot on Twin City soil they become the first women ever to be hailed as official delegates to such a conclave.

1893—Librarian Gratia Countryman of the Minneapolis Public Library opens the nation's first children's room designed for young readers of the Twin Cities and its environs. Of the fifteen hundred titles, *Little Lord Fauntleroy* by Frances Hodgson Burnett is the first to be chosen. Other popular volumes that enter circulation immediately include *The Wizard of Oz, The Jungle Book, Black Beauty, Peter Rabbit,* and *Alice in Wonderland.* Before the end of the decade, Countryman's radical innovation proves so successful that it is being imitated far and near.

1897—The legislature appropriates five thousand dollars as seed money to launch the Gillette State Hospital, designed to "provide for the care and treatment of deformed and crippled children." Like the library experiment four years earlier, this innovation is widely hailed and quickly copied in other states.

March 1898—Morris & Wilson of Minneapolis launch their *Book Index.* Library patrons can scan a list containing every book issued by a major publisher each month. At the end of the year, it is cumulated. Found to be so helpful, it becomes *Books in Print,* containing all American books currently available.

1898—Some Minnesota citizens are the first volunteers to fight against the Spanish in Cuba.

29

Matchless Minnesota

Twentieth-Century Firsts

1901—Uncertain as to whether long periods of reading may injure a person's eyesight, the legislature takes a preventive measure. Its optometry legislation is the first in the nation to establish legal standards for eye doctors.

1903—The Minneapolis Symphony Orchestra is organized and soon is recognized as one of the finest in the United States.

1905—At Duluth the predecessor of today's skylift goes into operation without a single delay or accident. A gigantic steel span built over the canal separating Duluth from Minnesota Point, it is touted as being capable of conveying up to six autos and "numerous passengers." Officially rated at a "burden capacity of 125,000 pounds," it is initially called "an aerial ferry." The completion of the 186-foot-tall conveyor is a first achievement by Minnesotans that fails to spawn imitators in other states.

1908—The Board of Regents of the University of Minnesota establishes a School of Nursing headed by Bertha Erdmann. Other land-grant universities in the nation follow suit.

1908—The village of Chisholm, with only three thousand citizens, becomes familiar everywhere because it is in the center of a region where four hundred thousand acres of fine trees are burned in a single day. This is a loss of at least two million dollars' worth of standing timber at a time when first-class postage is two cents.

1910—A successful device for "washing" iron ore is tried at Coleraine.

1910—At Split Rock on the northern shore of Lake Superior, close to the town of Two Harbors, the tallest lighthouse in the United States goes into operation. It guides ships until 1968.

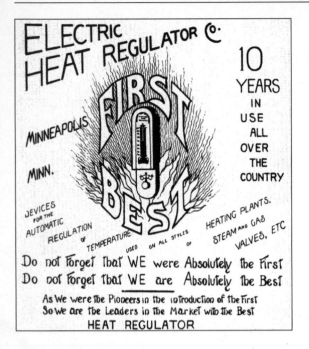

Shortly before the beginning of the 20th century, a few far-sighted Americans in other states were using Minnesota-made Electric Heat Regulators.

1913—At Minneapolis Dr. Gerald Bertram is the principal force behind the organization of America's first association of physicians with special interest in the use of vaccines. The society quickly goes national, and its members broaden their focus to include the entire field of immunology.

1915—The U.S. Patent Office recognizes Carl G. Muench as sole inventor of a brand-new kind of building material: tiny particles of wood bonded together to form what Muench calls Insulite, which substantially reduces echoes in large rooms. His mill at International Falls is the first in a now-vast industry devoted to sound-absorbing materials.

1920—An auto shop in Minneapolis gives a test run for the first fully protected armored commercial car, which is put into service by the Sweeney Detective Bureau of Saint Paul.

1920—A new political party, the Farmer-Labor Party, is founded in Minneapolis. Its outstanding leader is Floyd B. Olson, elected governor from 1931 to 1936. He is followed in office by fellow party members Hjalmer Peterson (1936–1937) and Elmer A. Benson (1937–1939). In 1944 the party merges with the Minnesota Democratic Party.

Split Rock lighthouse on Lake Superior was erected at a commanding height in order to give long-distance warning that Beaver Bay was rimmed with dangerous reefs. [MINNESOTA TOURIST BUREAU]

1922—At Babbitt, an experimental plant successfully concentrates low-grade iron ore called taconite, now a major raw material for the steel mills of the Western world.

1925—The Saint Louis County public library system puts into operation the first known bookmobile.

1926—In June the McGraw Electric Company of Minneapolis advertises the world's first electric toaster designed for household use for less than fifteen dollars.

1926—The Minnesota Mining and Manufacturing Company of Saint Paul launches experimental sales of a new product under the registered trade name of Scotch Tape. The patent for this pressure-sensitive transparent tape is not issued to inventor Richard G. Drew until 1930.

1927—The world's first Pullman car equipped with roller bearings "in which a sleeping person seems almost to float on air" is put into service between the Twin Cities and Chicago.

1929—William Watts Folwell, first president of the University of Minnesota, dies at age ninety-six. His four-volume *History of Minnesota* is still regarded as having no peer.

1932—For the first time in a presidential election, Minnesota gives its popular and electoral votes to a Democrat—Franklin D. Roosevelt.

1933—The nation's first comprehensive program designed to assist students who cannot afford to go to college is started.

1933—In the depths of the Great Depression, Minnesota law-makers adopt special "mortgage moratorium acts" designed to protect homeowners from foreclosure of their mortgages. When challenged, the legislation, is upheld by the Minnesota Supreme Court and then by the U.S. Supreme Court.

1935—Under the leadership of Gov. Floyd B. Olson and his Farmer-Labor Party, a state income tax is initiated. Called "one of the most progressive state tax structures in the nation," it is quickly imitated by other state legislative bodies.

1949—Minnesota Mining and Manufacturing Company engineers test a machine to mass-produce recordings on magnetic tapes. It puts two full days and nights of recorded music on tape during a single hour of operation.

1957—At Crosby a research balloon piloted by U.S. Air Force Maj. David G. Simons sets a new world record by reaching an altitude of 101,516 feet during the flight that ends at Elm Lake, South Dakota. Simons stayed aloft in the balloon for thirty-two hours.

*   *   *

At the University of Minnesota in Saint Paul, the world's largest collection of books by and about Scandinavians testifies that for decades persons from that part of the Old World flocked to the Land of Lakes in greater numbers than to any other American state.

*   *   *

Beginning about 1880 and continuing for a period of forty years, Minneapolis was literally "the flour capital of the world." Although many of its mills have disappeared, corporations such as General Mills that were originally flour-based companies are now multinational giants whose impact is global.

*   *   *

Using the best data then available, early Minnesotans con-cluded that there are about ten thousand separate bodies of water in the state. Hence the nickname "the Land of Ten Thousand Lakes" was coined. Geographers today have the advan-tage of photos made from satellites so it is now known that the land is dotted with nearly fifteen thousand lakes that are ten acres or larger in size. Collectively, the lakes of the state cover

In company with Queen Elizabeth II, Dwight D. Eisenhower came to Minnesota when the internationally significant St. Lawrence Seaway went into operation. [LIBRARY OF CONGRESS]

more than five thousand square miles—or 720,000 acres, not including the Minnesota portion of Lake Superior.

* * *

The most ambitious project of its kind ever undertaken had as a major result the transformation of Duluth into a world-class port despite the city's location nearly twenty-four hundred miles from the Atlantic Ocean. When it was opened for traffic, the international significance of the Saint Lawrence Seaway brought both President Dwight D. Eisenhower and Queen Elizabeth II to opening-day ceremonies. It took a few years for traffic to mount, but Duluth soon became the largest freshwater port in the world, a title it still maintains today.

* * *

The Mall of America in the Twin Cities is the largest covered shopping center on Earth.

* * *

With more than seventy-five units, the Minnesota State Parks system, totaling nearly two hundred thousand acres, is believed to be the most comprehensive in the United States.

*   *   *

Many persons seeking to find books' authors, titles, and publication data in order to request them from a local institution by interlibrary loan are astonished to discover that access to the University of Minnesota Libraries opens doors much wider than those of the Library of Congress. Once inside the Saint Paul collection, a researcher has instant access to the entire holdings of all universities numbered among "The Big Ten."

*   *   *

Some achievements are of such epochal proportions that they continue to be significant even when fresh innovations cause them to become obsolete. That is the case with a monumental breakthrough made by the Sperry Rand Corporation. With the world deeply interested in computers but uncertain about their capabilities, "thin-film memory" was developed at Saint Paul.

Gigantic by comparison with new generations of computers, Univac 1107 demonstrated that it is possible to store and retrieve immense amounts of information at a speed at least a thousand times faster than any other device that existed at the time. Though Univac is long gone except as a museum exhibit, this Minnesota-developed machine demonstrated that computers were here to stay and helped to spur the development of silicone chips that have replaced Univac's tape that was coated with minute particles of iron capable of responding to low-level magnetic impulses.

*   *   *

So many innovations have come from the Minneapolis-based Honeywell Corporation that the modern world would be quite different without them. Although it is inconspicuous by comparison with today's awesome technology, it's virtually certain that you are reading this book in a comfort zone that is provided by one of Honeywell's products—the thermostat, which, in its infancy more than a century ago, was called simply "the automatic regulator."

30
Mankato

Beginning of the End

On September 6, 1862, Gov. Alexander Ramsey dispatched an urgent telegram to the president of the United States: "This [Sioux uprising] is not our war. It is a national war. Answer me at once. More than 500 whites have been murdered by Indians."

Abraham Lincoln, who almost certainly realized that the withdrawal of U.S. Army troops from frontier posts had created a power vacuum that invited an Indian uprising, acted before nightfall. Creating the Military Department of the Northwest, he placed Maj. Gen. John Pope in command at Saint Paul.

Minnesotans did not wait for the arrival of the veteran who had already been in command in numerous major Civil War battles. Militiamen led by Col. Henry H. Sibley captured Red Iron's camp near the Chippewa River and released more than two hundred persons who had been held there as prisoners. Spurred forward by some of Sibley's men who had fought at Murfreesboro, Tennessee, and other battles as members of the Third Minnesota Regiment, Minnesotans began herding captured Sioux into hastily erected stockades. Before the end of October, an estimated two thousand Native American men, women, and children were being held under armed guard.

Individuals suspected of having taken part in the insurrection, Sibley wrote to a friend, would be tried before a special commission he expected soon to name. "If found guilty," he concluded, "they will be forthwith executed, although it will perhaps be a stretch of my authority. If so, necessity must be my justification." By then, his authority was much greater than

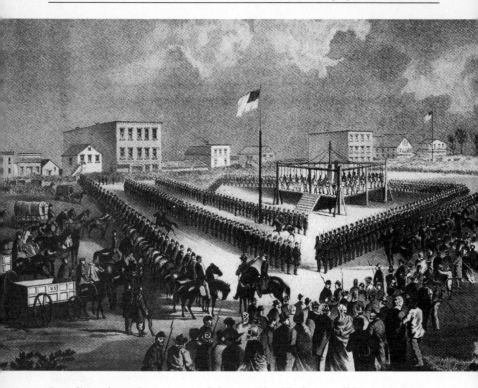

Long lines of armed men surrounded every side of the huge scaffold on which 38 men died in reprisal of the Sioux insurrection.

it had been earlier; as a reward for his leadership in mastering tribesmen of Minnesota, Lincoln had made him a brigadier general of volunteers.

Sibley selected five officers of the militia to form a commission that was not formally authorized: Col. William Crooks, Lt. Col. William R. Marshall, and Captains Hiram P. Grant, Hiram S. Bailey, and Rollin C. Olin. The court sat briefly at Camp Release, where many prisoners had been freed earlier. After a brief period there, the "justices" chose Mankato as their base but moved to Fort Snelling for the last of their hearings that extended through five weeks. According to contemporary newspaper accounts, 425 Sioux warriors were arraigned and given hearings sometimes lasting no more than five minutes. Eighteen warriors were found guilty of relatively minor charges, but 307 were condemned as murderers and sentenced to death.

When some of the condemned men were shipped through New Ulm, on the way to Mankato, the sight of the Indians so enraged the residents that some of them—mostly women wielding clubs and knives) attacked the wagons in which the Indians were chained together. Though a number of the prisoners were described as "battered and bruised," the list of condemned men was reduced by only one who was killed.

Meanwhile, in several major eastern cities, "a great outcry was raised that Minnesota was contemplating a dreadful massacre of Indians," one report stated. Responding to petitions sent to him, Lincoln requisitioned the records of the trial commission and turned them over to his legal aides. Following their advice, he reduced the number of men scheduled to die to thirty-nine—all of whom are named in President Lincoln's *Collected Works*.

On December 6, the president authorized the execution of the thirty-nine on the nineteenth day of the month. Simultaneously, he stipulated that the remaining prisoners must be held "subject to further orders, taking care that they neither escape nor are subjected to any unlawful violence." Three days later, having examined fresh evidence just received from Saint Paul, Lincoln notified Sibley to remove the name of "'Chaska-don' or 'Chaskay-etay,' alias Robert Hopkins" from the list of the condemned.

Sibley responded with an urgent plea plus a set of explanations. He needed an additional week to get ready for the execution "and for concentrating the troops necessary to protect the other Indians and preserve the peace," he wrote. According to the newly appointed general, "excitement prevails all sections of the state and secret combinations exist embracing thousands of citizens pledged to execute all the Indians." In this climate, he felt that delay was imperative and that "matters must be managed with great discretion and as much secrecy as possible to prevent a fearful collision between the U.S. forces and the citizens."

Lincoln having acceded to Sibley's request for a seven-day delay, according to the *Saint Paul Pioneer*, the Reverend Father Ravoux and assisting priests administered baptism to many of the condemned men on Christmas Day. Back at the stockade

Part of Red Cloud's 1870 delegation to Washington; Red Cloud sits in the middle.

on the following morning, Ravoux urged them to "hold out bravely and be strong, and show no sign of fear." Despite this exhortation, a warrior known only as "old Tazoo" broke out in "a death-wail, in which one after another joined, until the air was filled with a wild, unearthly plaint, which was neither of despair nor grief, but rather a paroxysm of savage passion," the report said.

The prisoners were led onto the single huge gallows, and precisely at 10:00 A.M. the trapdoor was sprung and thirty-eight men were hanged. Hundreds of civilians came to see the bodies of the lifeless warriors swaying in the wind. It is doubtful that any of these onlookers or any members of the military units on guard realized that the spectacle symbolized the beginning of the end of a proud and long-powerful people.

As Sibley had feared, there was a "general uprising of citizens" seeking vengeance, and punitive military expeditions were launched against the Sioux, who had fled into Dakota Territory. Sibley led one body of troops while another set out from

Maj. Gen. George Armstrong Custer, whose death at the Little Big Horn sealed the fate of all bands of Sioux.

"Sioux City on the Missouri River" under the leadership of Gen. Alfred Sully.

The three hundred warriors who had been condemned to die by the commission but who were reprieved by Washington remained imprisoned at Mankato throughout the long winter. They were then shipped down the Mississippi to Rock Island, where most of them remained about three years before being sent far to the West. Meanwhile, about seventeen hundred prisoners were herded into a stout compound at Fort Snelling, where they spent what many residents of the state branded "a most horrible winter." Soon after the spring thaw, most of these Sioux were forced aboard river steamers and taken to Crow Creek reservation on the Missouri River in South Dakota. A few years later their descendants and those who survived were shipped to a reservation close to Niobrara, Nebraska.

Oglala and other Teton Sioux had earlier migrated from Minnesota to the Missouri River basin and from that point to the Black Hills. At trading fairs, these western Sioux secured guns and other manufactured goods. In the decade following the great uprising in Minnesota, distant kinsmen of the insurgents chose Red Cloud as their leader and settled at the agency named for him. By the time the Wyoming Territory was formed in 1869, whites had already made plans to seek gold in regions set aside by Washington as Indian country.

President Ulysses S. Grant was besieged with demands that the Sioux should be confined to small reservations, but numerous prominent easterners were opposed to this policy. In this climate of divided public opinion, Red Cloud led a delegation of twenty-one persons to the nation's capital and secured promises of "many lavish gifts" plus vague assurances about the size and location of reservations.

Citing troubles in Minnesota, Gen. Philip Sheridan had secretly won the president's assent to placing Red Cloud's group and all three other Sioux agencies under military control. In the East, this drastic step was widely seen as the fulfillment of Minnesota's strident demand that every Sioux on the continent should be driven far from tribal lands and kept under strict supervision for all time to come.

Several years after the great Sioux uprising in Minnesota, no one there or anywhere else dreamed that before the decade ended, Indians would seek delayed reprisals. Their swift and unexpected actions led to the slaughter of George Armstrong Custer and many of his men in 1876 at the Little Bighorn River in Montana.

Conclusion

The pages of this volume do no more than scratch the surface of the saga of Minnesota and its people. To find out more about this fascinating state that has no equal among the other forty-nine, you may wish to devote some long winter nights—and maybe an exceptionally hot summer afternoon—in quest of more stories and curiosities.

Your local library includes a rich vein of information, and what's more, you can use a school or home or library computer to access libraries far and near to find titles of additional books you'd like to look at.

Once you have started a list of the books you would like to read, take it to your local library and request a few books on interlibrary loan. Some good starting places in a search for information about Minnesota and its people are

> The Minnesota Historical Society
> The Library of Congress
> University of Minnesota Libraries
> Amazon Books on the Internet
> Barnes and Noble, also on the Internet

If you decide you would like to know more about notable Minnesotans, you'll find that several encyclopedias include lists of them, as does *The World Almanac*, which lists states of birth for "Notable Living American Writers." Another long section dealing with "Entertainment Personalities" will tell you where each of the entertainers was born and when.

It's easy to look for "MN" in these and other lists.

Another good source of information is the "North Central" tour book published by the Automobile Association of America. The book is free to members and gives some of the highlights of

Minnesota as well as Iowa, Nebraska, South Dakota, and North Dakota.

Using these resources, *A Treasury of Minnesota Tales* can be your personal jumping-off place for fun, adventure, and learning about "matchless Minnesota."

Bibliography

Adams, Henry. *History of the United States During the Administration of Thomas Jefferson.* 2 vols. New York: Boni, 1930.

Adams, James Truslow. *The Living Jefferson.* New York: Harper, 1949.

Ambrose, Stephen E. *Undaunted Courage.* New York: Simon & Schuster, 1997.

Atkins, Annette. *Harvest of Grief—Grasshopper Plagues.* Saint Paul: Historical Society, 1984.

Arnason, David, and Vincent Arnason. *The New Icelanders.* N.p: Turnstone, 1994.

Bailey, John W. *Pacifying the Plains.* Westport: Greenwood, 1979.

Benton, Thomas H., *Decision of the Supreme Court of the United States in the Dred Scott Case.* New York: Appleton, 1857.

———. *Historical and Legal Examination of the Dred Scott Case.* New York: Appleton, 1938.

Blegen, Theodore C. *Minnesota.* Minneapolis: University of Minnesota Press, 1975.

———. *The Kensington Rune Stone.* St. Paul: Minnesota Historical Society, 1968.

Blum, Fred H. *Toward a Democratic Work Process.* New York: Harper, 1982.

Branch, E. Douglas. *The Hunting of the Buffalo.* Lincoln: University of Nebraska, 1962.

Brant, Marley. *Outlaws.* Montgomery, Alabama: Elliot and Clark, 1997.

Breihan, Carl W. *The Escapades of Frank and Jesse James.* New York: Fell, 1978.

Broadhead, James O. *The Louisiana Purchase.* St. Louis: Missouri Historical Society, 1897.

Brook, Michael. *Reference Guide to Minnesota History.* Saint Paul: Minnesota Historical Society, 1974.

Brown, Elton T. *A History of the Great Minnesota Forest Fires.* St. Paul: n.p., 1894.

Brown, Everett S. *The Constitutional History of the Louisiana Purchase.* Berkeley: University of California Press, 1920.

Bryant, Charles S., and Abel B. Murch. *A History of the Great Massacre by the Sioux Indians.* Millwood, N.Y.: Kraus, 1977.

Buck, Solon J. *The Granger Movement.* Cambridge: Harvard University Press, 1913.

Burns, Virginia. *Lewis Cass.* Bath, Mich.: Enterprise Press, 1980.

Burt, Olive. *John Charles Frémont.* New York: Messner, 1955.

Cantor, George. *Historic Festivals.* Detroit: Gale Research, 1996.

Carroll, Francis M. and Franklin R. Raiter. *Fires of Autumn.* Saint Paul: Minnesota Historical Society, 1990.

Catlin, George. *Letters and Notes on the North American Indians.* 2 vols. Reprint, New York: J. G. Press, 1995.

Chidsey, Donald B. *Lewis and Clark.* New York: Crown, 1970.

Coleman, Emily R. *The Complete Judy Garland.* New York: Harper and Row, 1990.

Coues, Elliott. *The Expeditions of Zebulon Montgomery Pike.* 2 vols. New York: Dover, 1987.

Darling, Arthur B. *Our Rising Empire.* New Haven: Yale University Press, 1940.

Davis, Kenneth S. *The Hero: Charles A. Lindbergh.* Garden City: Doubleday, 1959.

Dillon, Richard. *Meriwether Lewis.* New York: Coward-McCann, 1965.

Donald, Jay. *Outlaws of the Border.* Cincinnati: Forshee and McMakin, 1882.

The Dred Scott Papers. Columbia, Mo.: Missouri Historical Society, 1949.

Duluth News Tribune, 1894.

Dunbar, Willis F. *Lewis Cass.* Grand Rapids: Eerdmans, 1970.

Ellis, Richard N. *General Pope and U. S. Indian Policy.* Alburquerque: University of New Mexico Press, 1976.

Eastman, Mary Henderson. *Dahcotah.* New York: Wiley, 1849.

Ellis, Horace J. *The Wizard of Oz.* New York: Grossett and Dunlap, 1976.

Emmett, Boris and John E. Jeuck. *Catalogues and Counters—A*

History of Sears, Roebuck, and Company. Chicago: University of Chicago Press, 1950.

Fehrenbacher, Don E. *The Dred Scott Case.* New York: Oxford University Press, 1978.

————. *Slavery, Law, and Politics.* New York: Oxford University Press, 1981.

Finch, Christopher. *Rainbow: The Stormy Life of Judy Garland.* New York: Grossett and Dunlap, 1975.

Fleischner, Jennifer. *The Dred Scott Case.* Brookfield, Conn.: Millbrook Press, 1997.

Franklin, John H. *From Slavery to Freedom.* New York: Knopf, 1967.

Frémont, J. C. *The Exploring Expedition to the Rocky Mountains.* Washington, D.C.: Blair and Rives, 1845.

Furtwangler, Albert. *Acts of Discovery.* Urbana: University of Ill. Press, 1993.

Gayarre, Charles. *History of Louisiana.* 4 vols. New York: Middleton, 1866.

Gill, Brendan. *Charles A. Lindbergh.* New York: Harcourt Brace Jovanovich, 1959.

Gjevre, John A. *Saga of the Soo.* LaCrosse, Wisc.: Molzahn, 1973.

Goodrich, Thomas. *Scalp Dance.* Harrisburg, Pa.: Stackpole, 1997.

Gray, Edward F. *Leif Eriksson.* New York: Oxford University Press, 1930.

Green, Hardy. *On Strike at Hormel.* Philadelphia: Temple University Press, 1990.

Gump, James O. *The Dust Rose Like Smoke.* Lincoln: University of Nebraska Press, 1994.

Hage, Dave, and Paul Klauda. *No Retreat, No Surrender.* New York: Morrow, 1989.

Harnsberger, John L. "Jay Cooke and Minnesota." Ph.D. diss., University of Minnesota, 1956.

Harper's Encyclopedia of United States History. 10 vols. New York: Harper, 1905.

Hear the Future. Minneapolis: Minnesota Public Radio, 1996.

Herda, D. J. *The Dred Scott Case.* Hillside, N.J.: Enslow, 1994.

Herrick, C. L. *The Mammals of Minnesota.* Minneapolis: Harrison and Smith, 1892.

Hoffman, Daniel. *Paul Bunyan.* Lincoln: University of Nebraska Press, 1983.

Holand, Hjalmar R. *Westward from Vinland*. New York: Dover, 1940.

Holbrook, Stewart. *Lost Men of American History*. New York: Macmillan, 1946.

Holmes, Frank L. *Minnesota in Three Centuries*. 4 vols. N.p.: 1908.

Hough, Louis. *The Boundaries of the Louisiana Purchase*. Saint Louis: Roeder, 1901.

Howard, Benjamin C. *The Decision of the Supreme Court in the Case of Dred Scott*. Washington, D.C.: Wendell, 1857.

Huntington, George. *Robber and Hero*. Northfield, Minn.: Christian Way, 1895.

Hyde, George E. *Red Cloud's Folks*. Norman: University of Oklahoma Press, 1937.

Jarchow, Merrill E. *The Earth Brought Forth—A History of Minnesota Agriculture*. Saint Paul: Minnesota Historical Society, 1949.

Jensen, Derrick. *Railroads and Clearcuts*. Spokane: Inland Empire Public Lands, 1995.

Josephy, Alvin M., Jr. *War on the Frontier*. Alexandria, Va.: Time-Life, 1986.

Juneau, James. *Judy Garland*. New York: Pyramid, 1974.

Lamppa, Marvin. *Mesabi Iron Ranges*. Eveleth, Minn.: Lamppa, 1977.

Larsen, Lawrence H. *Wall of Flames*. Fargo: North Dakota State University, 1984.

Larson, Agnes M. *History of the White Pine Industry in Minnesota*. Reprint, New York: Arno, 1972.

Larson, Bruce. *Lindbergh of Minnesota*. New York: Harcourt Brace Jovanovich, 1973.

Latham, Frank B. *The Dred Scott Decision*. New York: Watts, 1968.

Laut, A. C. *Pathfinders of the West*. New York: Macmillan, 1918.

Lewis, Meriwether. *Original Journals of the Lewis and Clark Expedition*. Boston: Houghton, Mifflin, 1953.

Lincoln, Abraham. *Collected Works*. Edited by Roy P. Basler. 9 vols. New Brunswick: Rutgers University Press, 1953–55.

Lindbergh, Charles A. *Autobiography of Values*. New York: Harcourt Brace Jovanovich, 1978.

————. *Boyhood on the Upper Mississippi*. Saint Paul: Minnesota Historical Society, 1972.

————. *The Spirit of St. Louis*. New York: Scribner's, 1953.

————. *Wartime Journals*. New York: Harcourt Brace Jovanovich, 1970.

————. *We*. New York: Putnam's, 1927.

Long, Stephen H. *The Northern Expeditions of Stephen H. Long*. Saint Paul: Minnesota Historical Society, 1978.

Longfellow, Henry W. *The Song of Hiawatha*. Philadelphia: Henry Altemus, 1898.

————. *The Song of Hiawatha*. Cleveland: World, 1889.

Love, Robertus. *The Rise and Fall of Jesse James*. Lincoln: University of Nebraska Press, 1990.

Luckett, Perry D. *Charles A. Lindbergh*. New York: Greenwood, 1986.

Ludvigsen, Karl, and David B. Wise. *Complete Encyclopedia of the American Automobile*. Secaucas, N.J.: Chartwell, n.d.

McLaughlin, Andrew C. *Lewis Cass*. New York: Chelsea House, 1980.

Malone, Dumas. *Jefferson and His Time*. 6 vols. Boston: Little, Brown, 1970–81.

Meltzer, Milton, and Walter Harding. *A Thoreau Profile*. Concord, Mass.: Thoreau Foundation, 1962.

Mickelson, Sig. *The Northern Pacific Railroad*. Freeman, S.D.: Pine Hill, 1993.

Minneapolis Tribune, 1872–96.

Mohr, Howard. *A Minnesota Book of Days*. New York: Penguin, 1989.

Morella, Joe. *Judy: The Films and Career of Judy Garland*. New York: Citadel, 1969.

Morrill, Madge H. *Explorers to the West*. Nashville: Abingdon, 1962.

National Cyclopedia of American Biography. Ann Arbor, Mich.: University Microfilms, 1967ff.

"The Northfield Bank Raid." *Northfield News*, 1926.

Oehler, C. M. *The Great Sioux Uprising*. New York: Oxford University Press, 1959.

Page One—Major Events, 1920–75 as Presented in the New York Times. New York: Arno, 1975.

Rachleff, Peter. *Hard-Pressed in the Heartland*. Boston: South End, 1993.

Radisson, Pierre Esprit. *Voyages*. New York: B. Franklin, 1971.

Richardson, Robert D. *Henry Thoreau*. Berkeley: University of California Press, 1994.

Rogers, D. Laurence. *Paul Bunyan*. Bay City, Mich.: Historical Press, 1993.

Ross, Walter S. *The Last Hero—Charles A. Lindbergh*. New York: Harper and Row, 1976.

Rounds, Glen. *Ol' Paul, the Mighty Logger*. New York: Holiday, 1976.

Saint Paul Daily Globe, 1875.

Saint Paul Pioneer Press, 1872.

Sanders, Coyne S. *Rainbow's End: the Judy Garland Show*. New York: Morrow, 1990.

Schanzer, Rosalyn. *How We Crossed the West*. Washington: National Geographic, 1997.

Schleuning, Neala J. *Women, Community, and the Hormel Strike of 1985*. N.p.: Women's Studies, 1994.

Schorger, A. W. *The Passenger Pigeon*. Norman: University of Oklahoma Press, 1974.

Schrader, Del. *Jesse James Was One of His Names*. Arcadia, Calif.: Santa Anita, 1975.

Schreiner, Samuel A. *Henry Clay Frick*. New York: St. Martin's, 1995.

Schutz, Wallace J., and Walter N. Trenerry. *Abandoned by Lincoln-General John Pope*. Urbana: University of Illinois Press, 1990.

Sears, Roebuck Catalogue. 1897.

———. 1902.

———. 1927.

Shipman, David. *Judy Garland*. New York: Hyperion, 1992.

Smalley, Eugene V. *History of the Northern Pacific Railroad*. New York: Putnam's, 1883.

Steele, Phillip W. and George Warfel. *The Many Faces of Jesse James*. Gretna, La.: Pelican, 1995.

Thomson, George M. *Warrior Prince: Rupert of the Rhine*. London: Secker and Warburg, 1976.

Thoreau, Henry D. *Journal*. 14 vols. Reprint, New York: Dover, n.d.

Thorndike, Thaddeus. *Lives and Exploits of Frank and Jesse James*. Bowie, Md.: Heritage, 1992.

Torme, Mel: *The Other Side of the Rainbow*. London: Allen, 1971.

Triplett, Frank, comp. *The Life, Times, and Treacherous Death of Jesse James*. Chicago: Swallow, 1970.

Untermeyer, Louis. *The Wonderful Adventures of Paul Bunyan.* New York: Limited Editions Club, 1945.

Vexler, Robert I., ed. *Chronology & Documentary Handbook of Minnesota.* Dobbs Ferry, N.Y.: Oceana, 1978.

Wheeler, Olin D. *Trail of Lewis and Clark.* 2 vols. New York: Putnam's, 1904.

Wilson, Charles M. *The Dred Scott Decision.* Philadelphia: Auerbach, 1973.

Index

Boldface page numbers indicate illustrations.